ALCOHOLISM AND
DRUG ABUSE
IN THE WORKPLACE

ALCOHOLISM AND DRUG ABUSE IN THE WORKPLACE

Managing Care and Costs Through
Employee Assistance Programs

Second Edition

Walter F. Scanlon

New York
Westport, Connecticut
London

Library of Congress Cataloging-in-Publication Data

Scanlon, Walter F.
    Alcoholism and drug abuse in the workplace : managing care and
costs through employee assistance programs / Walter F. Scanlon. —
2nd ed.
       p.   cm.
    Includes bibliographical references and index.
    ISBN 0-275-93675-9 (alk. paper). — ISBN 0-275-93676-7 (pbk. :
alk. paper)
    1. Employee assistance programs. 2. Alcoholism and employment.
3. Drugs and employment.   I. Title.
HF5549.5.E42S37   1991
658.3'822—dc20   90-49202

British Library Cataloguing in Publication Data is available.

Library of Congress Catalog Card Number: 90-49202
ISBN: 0-275-93675-9 (hb.)
      0-275-93676-7 (pbk.)

First published in 1991

Praeger Publishers, One Madison Avenue, New York, NY 10010
An imprint of Greenwood Publishing Group, Inc.

Printed in the United States of America

The paper used in this book complies with the
Permanent Paper Standard issued by the National
Information Standards Organization (Z39.48-1984).

10 9 8 7 6 5 4 3 2 1

To
Freedom
With Love

Contents

Preface

> Morality, to have any meaning at all, must be a principle of action. It must not be exhortation, sermon, or good intentions. It must be practices.
>
> Peter F. Drucker

The world of work and the world of counseling are not so far apart. Counseling, in fact, has always been a function of supervision, and effective human resource management requires training in both human relations and communications. While technical skills are most important to lower management levels, and conceptual skills are most important to upper management levels, human skills are essential on all levels of management. The ability to work with and understand people is as important to the CEO as it is to the plant supervisor. Unit chiefs, department heads, division managers, team leaders, vice presidents, general managers, and front-line supervisors all have one thing in common: They spend a great deal of time communicating, supervising, and negotiating with people. They become quite good at knowing what to say, who to say it to, and when to say it. They are effective observers of people and can quickly assess an environment to determine how best to manage that environment.

People who manage people have an endless flow of problems to solve that require procedural knowledge as well as good judgment. Any skilled manager or supervisor will know when an employee is not meeting performance standards, but knowing what to do with this information is not always obvious. Some supervisors will go by the book and impose disciplinary measures as per organization procedures while other supervisors might attempt to resolve problems informally. Either or both practices can be employed effectively, depending upon the skill of the supervisor and the structure of the organization. Some problems, however, may call for a different kind of action. Deteriorating job performance resulting from personal problems requires special handling and specific skills. Developing these skills, and learning what to do with them are not difficult tasks. A well-managed employee assistance program (EAP), among its other functions, provides both training and consultation services for supervisors and management staff. Most important, the EAP is a resource for the supervisor who has identified a performance problem that might prove to be indicative of a personal problem. Without an EAP such problems may be handled awkwardly or not at all. With an EAP in place, however, the solution may be a matter of following procedure. The procedure is, in effect, a cost-effective, early intervention management strategy designed to help employees with personal problems that interfere with their ability to function on the job. These problems are more often than not related to the use and abuse of alcohol and other drugs. The EAP objective is to reduce both the incidence of such problems and the costs associated with them.

Strategic intervention is, in fact, the focus of this book. In management terms, a strategic control point is where errors are caught before they become serious and costly problems. This may be any place along an assembly line, any step within the decision-making process, or any point in an employee's work performance. The control point here is, obviously, whenever the employee's performance begins to deteriorate. Realistically, however, intervention is not possible until a pattern of deteriorating job performance is established. The strategy, then, is a timely intervention and referral to the company employee assistance program. This book will provide the reader with an understanding of this strategy as applied to employees whose ability to function on the job has deteriorated because of personal problems.

The term "troubled employee" as used throughout this book refers specifically to those employees who are identified as having alcohol or other drug problems. This is a departure from the more typical usage where troubled employee could include employees with *any* personal problems. Similarly, "employee assistance program" as used throughout this book means any EAP staffed to work with the chemically dependent employee whether or not that is the *only* service that the program provides. A program staffed to help only alcohol-dependent employees, for example, will not be referred to as an employee alcoholism program. It will be called an employee assistance program.

The narrower application of these terms serves to eliminate awkward phrases such as "the alcoholism and drug abuse function of the employee assistance program," or "the troubled employee suffering from alcoholism or other drug abuse problems." In those rare instances where the terms "troubled employee" or "employee assistance program" are used in their generic forms, this will be indicated or will be implicit in the text.

The concept and practice of employee assistance programming is not limited to the United States. Many work organizations in developed and developing countries have recognized the importance of early identification of the chemically dependent person in the workplace. The Employee Assistance Professionals Association, Inc. (EAPA), has local chapters in several countries, and EAPA membership includes organizations and individuals from many countries. The research that made this book possible, unless otherwise noted, however, is limited to information collected from sources and studies on programs, organizations, and people in the United States. While much of the information herein might be applicable to organizations in other countries, differences in culture, governmental regulations, and societal mores should be taken into consideration.

The word "corporate" as used throughout this book applies to any work-organization—business, public, or voluntary—where an employee assistance program might be found. The term "corporate setting," therefore, means any organization—business or non-profit—where people are employed. "Corporation," "organization," "company," "firm," and "work-organization" are used interchangeably throughout.

The term "chemically dependent" as applied throughout this book means only those persons who are in the workplace today and those who will be in the workplace in the future. Since "chemical dependency" is a relatively new concept in referring to alcohol- and drug-abusing persons, it will not be used when discussing information of a historical nature. Alcoholism, drug abuse, and so on will be used in those instances. When applicable, all forms identifying the abuser of mood-altering substances may be used interchangeably, such as, chemical dependence and alcohol/drug dependence.

In researching that information necessary to the discussion on confidentiality, discrimination, and other legal aspects of employee assistance programming, I found that many legal questions were unresolved. I also discovered some contradictions in definitions and interpretations of guidelines and regulations protecting employee and patient rights. In discussing these matters with legal advisers, I was advised to present arguments in general terms and not attempt to solve or resolve these problems. I took their advice. Even experts in the field of employee assistance programming were cautious when discussing what a work-organization could do and could not do.

Sensitive matters such as screening employees for drug use, for example, was considered by some to be a therapeutic tool and by others to be a violation of civil rights. Organizations using such methods to minimize the use of drugs and alcohol in the workplace emphasized the need for written policies and proven procedures. In terms of legal compliance with guidelines that were less ambiguous, the issue of jurisdiction became a moot point. Compliance with federal and/or local statutes was contingent upon funding, taxes, number of employees, geographical location, and so on. With this understanding of the limitations of the legal issues to be discussed, it is hoped that the reader will not apply this information without first conducting research based on his or her corporate, union, or individual situation. The information provided here is intended to provoke thought and open the door to further research.

On the subject of research, the search for information that would eventually make this book possible began in my own small library of books, brochures, bulletins, handbooks, pamphlets, encyclopedias, newspapers, newsletters, periodicals, journals, and reports.

First, I divided the subject of the book into workable segments:

1. The concept of employee assistance programming.
2. The history of employee assistance programming.
3. The history of drug and alcohol use in the United States.
4 Current drug and alcohol use in the United States.
5. The legal, corporate, societal, and individual influences on rehabilitation and employee assistance programming.
6. Governmental influences, including the Drug-Free Workplace Act and mandatory drug screening.
7. Cost considerations, including the trend toward managed health care.

Then, after a thorough search and sorting out of the information I had on hand, I used references cited in these works to further my research. The indexes to business and consumer periodicals were included in my search for relevant and timely information, and computer searches by national clearinghouses were also conducted.

Primary sources of current information were contacted, such as the National Council on Alcoholism and Drug Dependence, the Alcoholism Council of Greater New York, the New York State Division of Substance Abuse Services, the Division of Alcoholism and Alcohol Abuse, the National Institute on Alcohol Abuse and Alcoholism, the National Institute on Drug Abuse, the Employee Assistance Professional Association, the National Association of Addiction Treatment Providers, and the National Association of State Alcohol and Drug Abuse Directors. Local councils, state agencies, and independent research groups throughout the country were generous with both time and information. Printed and verbal information was secured from these organizations and leads to other sources of information became available. For legal information my primary research sources were the Legal Action Center located in New York City and Washington, D.C., the American Civil Liberties Union, and whatever printed information could be found on the subjects of employee assistance programming and chemical dependency. Personal contacts with managers and directors of employee assistance programs and chemical dependency treatment programs were important primary sources of information.

Finally, both my early personal experience as a "troubled employee" and later as a professional in the field of employee assistance programming provided me the impetus, motivation, and knowledge to write such a book. In 1961 I was fired by a trade publication after several years of deteriorating job performance that was alcohol and drug related. Once unemployed, my chances of recovery diminished and the progression of the illness eventually rendered me unemployable. For the next nine years I remained unemployable, was totally dependent on alcohol and other drugs, and would be chemical-free only when under lock and key. Had it not been for the countless hospitalizations and institutionalizations, I probably would not be around to tell about it. In one such institution I learned about a program that could help me with my problem. In September 1969 my recovery began and has continued through today, alcohol- and drug-free since that date. After several years of abstinence, I trained as a counselor and entered the field of alcoholism and drug abuse treatment, eventually moving into program management and finally into the occupational sector and employee assistance programming. I am presently a management consultant.

I often wonder what might have happened if that trade publication that I worked for had had an employee assistance program. Would I have been referred to such a program and might it have spared me those nine years of degradation and deprivation? For me things turned out well after all. I survived. But the employer was not so lucky; the publication lost a potentially good employee. That was 1961, a time when there were only fifty employee assistance programs in operation nationally. Today there are better than 20,000 such programs, an indication that work organizations are catching on. The chance that a troubled employee will be identified and referred for assistance today is far greater than it was then. This alternative to firing continues to grow, yet many organizations elect not to install EAPs. This book will, I hope, provide enough information to place the issue in its proper perspective and allow the reader to decide which is the best alternative, termination or intervention. The writer's bias will, inevitably, manifest itself.

Acknowledgments

Many colleagues, associates and friends, wittingly and unwittingly, made this book possible. Taking an idea and turning it into a readable document is a process requiring the input of many people. This input comes in the form of both hands-on assistance and moral support. It comes directly from those who made contributions in the form of labor, suggestions, and criticisms, and indirectly from those whose support and encouragement got me over the rough spots.

I am especially grateful to the EAP and MAP managers, treatment program directors, EAP consultants, personnel managers, medical personnel, and research staff members who contributed their expertise, experience, and time unselfishly so that this effort would be a timely one. Special appreciation goes to the New York City Chapter of the Employee Assistance Professionals Association and those members whose professional and personal support was there when I needed it.

Several people were especially important to both the motivating and writing processes that eventually took on the form of a book. They include David Shay for his contributions to Chapter 5, Marcie Bensman for her research on treatment costs and Gerda Steel for her support on this and past projects. They also include Anita Yulsman, whose involvement in the project from its earliest beginnings and her encouragement throughout the process deserve special appreciation.

Finally, I am particularly indebted to Kathleen Sullivan for her support throughout this project. Her time spent reviewing drafts spared prospective readers needless redundancy and brought organization and continuity to the manuscript. Had it not been for her council on member assistance programming and managed health care, the reader would have been deprived of key concepts in these and related areas.

The Scope and Cost of Chemical Dependency

Employee drug abuse and alcoholism is estimated to cost U.S. business and industry billions of dollars each year. A government-sponsored study by the Research Triangle Institute shows that the cost of reduced productivity alone is over $99 billion annually. An additional $17 billion is spent on treatment and support services. To give these otherwise incomprehensible figures some perspective, the combined cost amounts to $318 million per day or $13 million per hour![1]

Other sources fix the annual economic cost for alcohol abuse and dependence at $136 billion in 1990 and project $150 billion in 1995.[2, 3] Direct and indirect losses including treatment and productivity costs, no matter who is doing the counting, are always in the billions of dollars. Complete agreement on the actual cost of alcoholism and drug abuse to business and industry is, of course, impossible. The bottom line figure depends on the variables, formulas, and methods employed in the study. Yet, different studies are seldom far apart in their findings. Whatever the actual cost, all agree it is considerable. These corporate and government workplace expenses are ultimately passed on to the consumer through higher prices, taxes, and the high cost of health care. Based on the most recent statistics from the Department of Labor, if this expense were shared equally, it would cost each working person in the United States $843 annually.[4]

Federal drug-control agencies have always kept a watchful eye on the trafficking and distribution of illegal substances. They have maintained a safe distance, however, from the workplace and its problems with chemically dependent employees. The growing seriousness of this problem in recent years is changing that. Workplace chemical dependency, an integrative term identifying drug and alcohol abuse as two sides of the same coin, now has the attention of the government. Legislation and federal regulations, including the federal Drug-Free Workplace Act, are evidence of that. Focusing specifically on the use of controlled substances, recent government efforts to address it include the Bush administration's 1990 National Drug Control Strategy (Strategy II).[5] This is an aggressive action to reduce supply and availability, provide treatment, discourage drug use through education, and enforce the laws against drug violators. Many governmental agencies are also screening for drug use among their employees in safety-sensitive positions. The government is now taking an aggressive position in its effort to rid the workplace of drugs.

The impact of drug abuse on business and industry is not a new phenomenon. A report published in the Harvard Business Review in 1982 alerted us to a growing problem at that time:

> From the mailroom of the Justice Department to auto assembly plants, the community problems have found their way into the workplace. The use of drugs in the workplace is a serious and growing problem reflecting a national trend, but it is one that business generally ignores.[6]

One thing has changed. The drug problem is no longer ignored. A drug-free workplace is not only desirable in the 1990s; for some organizations it is the law. Private sector business organizations receiving federal government funding and grants must be in compliance if they expect to stay in business (see Chapter 4). For those organizations not required to comply, reduced productivity costs and treatment benefits costs call for decisive action (see Chapter 6).

The growth of the problem is evident in the number of treatment and ancillary services aimed at finding its solution. Ten years ago there were a fraction of the more than eight thousand inpatient and outpatient, drug and alcohol treatment programs we have today. This includes public and private sector facilities.[7] Related growth professions such as employee assistance consulting services, laboratories for drug screening, and programs that insure Drug-Free Workplace Act certification have also emerged. With this expansion of direct and indirect services comes an increase in treatment costs. This trend continues into the 1990s with 40 percent of the employer's total health care costs going to psychiatric and substance abuse benefits.[8] Also expected to continue is the growth of service companies prepared to reduce these costs, for a fee, through managed health care.

Recent studies suggest a decrease in drug use in the United States. The rate of growth in terms of new drug users has also decreased. This information needs to be qualified. First, it is important to note that many studies focus on high school students. The results of such studies are questionable in that drug users often drop out of school. Second, drug awareness and education programs have been somewhat successful in reducing the number of light drug users and discouraging new drug users. These facts notwithstanding, the hundreds of thousands of tons of cocaine and heroin arriving in the United States every year are proof that we have a serious problem. These drugs, and other mood-altering substances, are finding their way into the workplace.

Information becomes increasingly available to the general public as drug and alcohol abuse impacts on society and business. The proliferation of stories and articles in newspapers and magazines across the country is indicative of a serious rather than a casual interest in the subject. Articles in trade publications and business magazines are evidence that drug and alcohol-related problems continue to be a corporate and government concern. The all-too-familiar refrain, "We don't have such problems in this organization," is yesterday's joke. When heard today, it's with tongue firmly planted in cheek. The problem may be found on all levels of the organization and does not distinguish between men and women. Studies show that women, in fact, account for one-third of all cocaine users needing treatment. Most of these women, like the men, are in the workplace.

As history shows, there is no one solution to the problem. Legislation, interdiction, and law enforcement have been less than effective in reducing drug use to a manageable social concern. The demand is too great, the treatment too limited and the supply side too aggressive to contain the lucrative business of drug distribution. While the current administration's "war on drugs" is a noble effort, work organizations and labor unions have the real power to effect lasting change. The drug consumer is in the workplace, not on the street. While helping the street addict remains a social priority, it is the employed drug addict who keeps the cartels and distributors in business. From a social perspective, it remains the responsibility of business and labor to make a serious commitment toward finding a solution. It is from a cost perspective, however, that the impetus to rid the workplace of drug and alcohol abuse will come. The cost of not taking action is far greater than that of investing in a drug-free workplace. Educating and training the workforce, its supervisors, and management personnel is an important start. Many organizations are doing at least that much. Testing for drugs and taking disciplinary action, when indicated, may also be necessary. A well-designed benefits package and managed-care component should also be a part of the plan.

Reducing the high cost of drug and alcohol abuse involves a total commitment to that goal. The employee assistance program is the cornerstone of this commitment. While a "drug-free" workplace is not realistic, the key to managing the problem is in acting as if it is. This means identifying chemical dependency before it becomes a costly problem. The EAP remains the only department in an organization capable of effecting this objective.

NOTES

1. Research Triangle Institute, updated costs based on 1983 study, March 21, 1990.

2. National Council of Alcoholism and Drug Dependence, "Estimated Cost of Alcoholism to Business and Industry for 1990," (June 1990).

3. U.S. Department of Health and Human Services, National Institute on Alcohol Abuse and Alcoholism, "Seventh Special Report to the U.S. Congress on Alcohol and Health," 1990, 17.

4. U.S. Department of Labor, Bureau of Labor Statistics, Office of Employment and Unemployment Statistics, Division of Occupational and Administrative Statistics, "The Employment Situation," Washington D.C., USDL89-528, October 1989.

5. The National Institute on Drug Abuse, "A New Horizon/Drugfree Workplace Goals Can Eliminate the Problem of Drugs," *Employee Assistance* 2, No. 8 (March 1990): 16.

6. Peter B. Bensinger, "Drugs in the Workplace," *Harvard Business Review* (November–December 1982): 48–60.

7. *National Drug and Alcoholism Treatment Unit Survey (NDATUS), 1987, Final Report*, National Institute on Drug Abuse, National Instutute on Alcohol Abuse and Alcoholism (Rockville, MD: DHHS Publication No. 89–1626, 1989), 18, 19 Note: Estimates based of projection of outpatient and inpatient against private for-profit and non-profit total units.

8. "Cost Containment Through Outpatient Substance Abuse Services," *Employee Benefits Journal* 15, No. 1 (March 1990): 6–10.

2

Chemical Dependency: The Person, the Definition, the History

WHO IS THE CHEMICALLY DEPENDENT PERSON?

Substance abusers are not always easy to recognize. The alcoholic or drug abuser whose comical or tragic behavior immediately identifies the problem is likely to be unemployable, and searching for this person in the workplace would be less than productive. The flask-toting, happy-go-lucky, stereotypic "town drunk" and his drug-shooting counterpart, the romanticized "man with the golden arm" have not worked in years. Those who have managed to hold onto their jobs are a small part of the big problem, and while their problem cannot be ignored, they are the tip of the iceberg.

Most managers know this. Efforts to paint a more realistic picture of the chemically dependent person, including the identification of celebrities in recovery, have served to better educate the public. Yet the less enlightened continue to associate the alcoholic with skid row and the drug abuser with violence. Some drug abusers do commit crimes and some alcoholics can be found on skid row, but most are right in the mainstream. Only about three percent of the problem drinkers are on skid row or have skid-row lifestyles; the remaining 97 percent are living "normal" lives and can be found right in the workplace. There are an estimated 10.5 million Americans that exhibit some symptoms of alcoholism or alcohol dependence.[1] This fact is not news. Many companies have, in fact, made reference to this in their policies on employee alcohol and drug problems. The Mobil Oil Corporation, for example, addressed the problem of stereotyping in its manual almost fifteen years ago:

One of the chief problems in dealing with alcoholism and drug abuse is the elimination of stereotyping ideas surrounding these conditions. The typical alcoholic is often erroneously conceived of as a skid-row derelict. Actually, only a very small proportion of alcoholics fall into this category. Most are average citizens. Many are employed.[2]

As for the drug abuser, even the hardcore street addict is not likely to commit violent crimes. With those isolated incidents involving drug-induced psychotic episodes notwithstanding, the addict is more likely to sell drugs, do burglaries, shoplift, or commit other non-confrontative crimes to secure money. But equally important, this type of drug abuser is in the minority. The majority of illicit drug users, 70 percent, are employed.[3] This means that of the 14.5 million Americans currently using drugs, more than 10.1 million are in the workplace. These employees are using a variety of mood-altering substances including marijuana, cocaine, heroin, hallucinogens, inhalants, or nonmedical use of psychotherapeutics.[4] These facts come as no surprise to those professionals responsible for treating chemically dependent persons. Many corporations, especially those with EAPs in place, are likely to be aware of the impact of these "others" on productivity and job performance. And, as discussed in professional literature and employer manuals, these are employees whose misuse of prescribed substances and/or recreational drug use has progressed to the point where their ability to function normally is impaired.

The stereotype of the drug abuser as a hardcore street addict is equally erroneous. The fact is that while the use of heroin has received much public attention, the misuse of certain prescribed medications by the average citizen is the more common drug problem. Physical and psychological dependencies on tranquilizers and stimulants pose health problems very similar to those of alcoholism. Furthermore, it is not uncommon for individuals to develop dual dependencies on alcohol and drugs.[5]

As noted above, this policy was formulated almost fifteen years ago, yet it reflects an enlightened approach to the problem. The chemically dependent person may be someone who discovered that two valiums are better than one or that the codeine prescribed for a toothache feels good even when there is no pain to kill.

While cocaine and marijuana are not likely to be prescribed by physicians, the abuse of these substances in today's society is not so different from misusing prescribed medications. The availability of these and other mood-altering substances has made recreational drug use as easy as ordering a drink. The same person, in fact, may order a drink, do a line of coke, smoke marijuana, and misuse valium.

THE CHANGING PROFILE

The drug abuser that we're talking about here is different from the one we thought we knew. Unlike the classic heroin user whose progression to the final stages of addiction could take as little as twenty months, or the traditional alcoholic who might survive for twenty years before "hitting the skids," the new chemically dependent person is likely to fall somewhere in between. The progression here is less predictable, and their profile defies existing stereotypic notions. The profile, in fact, is the profile of an executive, a secretary, a manager, a laborer, an office worker, or a telephone repair person. The age might be anywhere from sixteen to sixty. They may use cocaine, crack, ice, heroin, prescription drugs, or alcohol. He or she may be well-educated, or not. Race, religion, or sex are not major factors. Medical professionals, lawyers, and high-ranking politicians use drugs. Since a high percentage of substance abusers are employed, it follows that the user can purchase the drug right in the workplace. With a potential market of millions, the dealer does not have to look far for business. The business is right there in the workplace.

THE MEDICAL PROFESSION DEFINES ALCOHOL AND DRUG ABUSE

Managers and supervisors need not know the clinical features and behavioral dynamics of chemical dependency to address the problem in the workplace, yet when conducting training sessions on how to use the company EAP effectively, many such questions are asked. There is a curiosity about the disease concept of alcoholism and about the medical approach to treating drug abusers. Supervisors want to understand the difference between an alcoholic and a heavy drinker as well as the difference between a recreational drug user and a drug abuser. They want to be convinced that chemical dependency is, indeed, a medical problem amenable to treatment; that the EAP is not just another level of bureaucracy created to "protect" the nonproductive employee.

While there are almost as many definitions of chemical dependency as there are substances of abuse, here are some definitions referred to and accepted by the professional community. *The Merck Manual* offers the following:

"Alcoholism is considered a chronic illness of undetermined etiology with an insidious onset, showing recognizable symptoms and signs proportionate to its severity."[6]

The American Society of Addiction Medicine (ASAM) and the National Council on Alcoholism and Drug Dependence (NCADD) have adapted a revised definition of alcoholism. The revised 1990 definition reflects new information on alcoholism and supersedes the 1976 definition published in the *Annals of Internal Medicine*:

> Alcoholism is a primary, chronic disease with genetic, psychological, and environmental factors influencing its development and manifestations. The disease is often progressive and fatal. It is characterized by continuous or periodic: impaired control over drinking, preoccupation with the drug alcohol, use of alcohol despite adverse consequences, and distortions in thinking, most notably denial.[7]

"Loss of control" is the characteristic that separates the alcoholic from the nonalcoholic. While some alcoholics may argue that they do not get drunk every time they drink, their inability to *consistently* control their consumption is what makes them different from social drinkers. An alcoholic will have every good intention to leave a bar after a few drinks and go home and may, in fact, succeed on some occasions. But more often than not this willpower will prove no match for the insidious onset of the disease.

Drug dependence defies a single definition. Because there are different drugs having different effects, including alcohol, each drug type would have to be defined separately. *The Merck Manual*, however, does provide a general definition of addiction:

> Addiction refers to a style of living that includes drug dependence, generally both physical and psychologic, but mainly connotes continuing compulsive use and overwhelming involvement with a drug. Addiction additionally implies the risk of harm and the need to stop drug use, whether the addict understands and agrees or not.[8]

Other definitions of alcoholism and drug abuse are more simply stated:

> Alcoholism is a condition which is characterized, among other things, by the drinker's consistent inability to choose whether to drink at all, or to stop drinking when he or she has obviously had enough, and drug abuse is the use of a drug for other than

medicinal purposes which results in the impaired physical, mental, emotional, or social well-being of the user. Drug misuse is the unintentional or inappropriate use of prescription or over-the-counter drugs, with similar results.[9]

All drug dependencies, including alcoholism, are diseases. Alcoholism was declared a disease by the American Medical Association in 1956. In 1987 a second resolution became a landmark AMA policy. It reads:

RESOLVED, That the American Medical Association endorse the proposition that drug dependencies, including alcoholism, are diseases and that their treatment is a legitimate part of medical practice; and be it further

RESOLVED, That the AMA encourage individual physicians, other health professionals, medical and other health-related organizations, and government and other policy makers to become more well informed about drug dependencies, and to base their policies and activities on the recognition that drug dependencies are, in fact, diseases.[10]

THOSE WHO DO AND THOSE WHO DO NOT

Whichever definition of alcoholism and/or drug abuse one chooses, it would be safe to assume that the chemically dependent person did not intend to lose control. He or she probably drank or used drugs for the same effect that the social drinker or recreational drug user seeks. The difference between the two, as stated above, is that one can stop at any point and the other can not. In terms of the progression of chemical dependency, the first drink or use of drugs usually starts in a social setting. It might be at a party, at home, with a group of kids on the corner, or in a school bathroom. It could be a glass of wine, a can of beer, or a marijuana cigarette. For some, the new experience may not be a desirable one, and they are not likely to have another drink or drug until an appropriate occasion arises. They may elect not to drink at all. Others may have found the experience pleasurable, the "high" enjoyable, and the altered state of consciousness they experienced to be fun. They enjoyed the effect of the chemical but equally important, they also enjoyed the camaraderie that went along with the experience. They were likely to place the experience in its proper perspective and go on to the more important things in their lives.

For most people the first experience with mood-altering chemicals is hardly worth remembering. For others, however, the effect is dramatic. In recalling their first experience with drinking or using other drugs, many recovering chemically dependent people will say such things as, "It was like magic," "It made me feel wonderful," "It was like being born all over again," "It made me feel that my whole life had changed," or "I realized how easy it was to feel better than I had ever felt before."[11] With just one drink or drug, most chemically dependent persons will recall that it became possible to feel attractive, smart, important, witty, and powerful.[12] Conversely, alcoholics drink both to relieve painful feeling states and to manipulate the environment.[13] They drink to relieve the pain of not feeling attractive, important, witty, and so on, and to manipulate the environment so as to create the "illusion" that they are. They may, indeed, possess these qualities but not feel that they do.

Whatever the drug of choice may be—and alcohol *is* a drug—most chemically dependent persons will be found in the workplace. People have always used substances to alter their state of consciousness and people have always worked for a living. It is likely, then, that those experiencing a "dramatic" effect when first introduced to drugs or drinks will be working alongside those who placed little importance on the event.

SOCIAL DRINKS AND RECREATIONAL DRUGS ARE HERE TO STAY

Some social scientists view drug use as a cultural phenomenon. The use of drugs to alter consciousness is nothing new. It has been a feature of human life in all places on earth and in all ages of history. The only people lacking a traditional intoxicant were the Eskimos, who had the misfortune to be unable to grow anything and had to wait for white men to bring them alcohol. Alcohol has always been the most commonly used drug simply because it does not take much effort to discover that the consumption of fermented juices produces interesting variation from ordinary consciousness.[14]

There is little evidence that a greater percentage of Americans are now taking drugs than once did, only that there has been an increase in the use of illegal drugs. During the past three decades, many young people chose cocaine products, hallucinogens, synthetic substances, and marijuana over alcohol. The 1990s are showing a trend back to alcohol. Marijuana remains a popular drug among youth while more dangerous substances are falling off in usage. Alcohol continues to be the drug of choice among the general population.

Although many reports show more people are using drugs today, much of this can be attributed to more sophisticated measurement techniques. It might also be attributed to the fact that alcohol is often not considered when measuring drug usage. *Licit & Illicit Drugs*, a study conducted by Consumer Union in the early 1970s, reported that drugs of choice change with the times. There were, in fact, periods in American history where drug use was so common it was hardly considered a problem. Before the turn of the century physicians dispensed opiates directly to patients, drugstores sold them over the counter, and grocery and general stores stocked them on their shelves; drugs could be ordered by mail and there were countless patent medicines on the market containing opium and morphine which were sold under such names as Godfrey's Cordial, Mrs. Winslow's Soothing Syrup, and McMunn's Elixir of Opium.

Cocaine remained popular through this period and into the twentieth century:

By 1890, the addicting and psychosis-producing nature of cocaine was well understood in medical circles; yet for another twenty years it does not appear to have occurred to many people to demand a law against the drug. In the United States, cocaine was widely used not only in Coca-Cola but also in "tonics" and other patent medicines.[15]

EARLY LEGISLATION

Several major steps were taken early in this century to control the distribution and sale of opiates and cocaine in the United States. The first was in 1906 when Congress passed the first Pure Food and Drug Act. This act required that medicines containing opiates and certain other drugs must say so on their labels. The Harrison Narcotics Act of 1914, however, totally cut off the supply of legal opiates for addicts. In 1924 a law was enacted prohibiting the importation of heroin altogether, even for medicinal use.

Both local and federal statutes enacted since the Harrison Narcotics Act were aimed at controlling drug use and abuse in this country. There were also early attempts at treatment, including expensive private sanitariums and federally supported facilities such as Lexington Hospital in Kentucky. Methadone maintenance clinics are a viable treatment approach today, but few people are aware that opiate clinics dispensing heroin and morphine existed between 1912 and 1922.[16]

Widespread use of marijuana is a problem in the workplace today. It is the drug of choice among our youth, but this is not the first time in American history that "smoke" gained popularity. By the 1930s there were more than five hundred "tea pads" in New York City alone.[17] Ironically, it was a change in the laws rather than a change in drug preference that stimulated a large-scale marketing of marijuana for recreational use in the United States. The enactment of the Eighteenth Amendment and the Volstead Act of 1920 raised the price of alcoholic beverages and made them less accessible. Prohibition made the manufacture, sale, and transportation of intoxicating liquors illegal. This fact and the inferior quality of the alcoholic beverages that were available triggered a substantial commercial trade in marijuana for recreational use.[18] As in the buying and selling of any product, the economic laws of supply and demand prevailed. It became cheaper and safer to smoke pot than to drink booze.

Attempts at mandating sobriety and abstinence have had little success. In 1918, three years after the Harrison Narcotics Act was passed, a committee was appointed to look into what appeared to be a growing drug abuse problem. The committee found that illegal drugs, specifically opiates and cocaine, were being used by one million people, and the underground traffic in narcotics was about equal to the legitimate traffic. Organized smuggling rings had formed and drugs were entering the United states through seaports and across the Canadian and Mexican borders. Twenty surveyed cities had reported increased drug usage since the passage of the Harrison Narcotics Act.[19]

The Volstead Act did not fare any better. Prohibition, the enforcement mechanism for the Eighteenth Amendment, was impossible to enforce. The benefits of this piece of legislation were overshadowed by its dramatic failures:

> In American and intellectual life since Repeal, Prohibition, an attempt at a structural and societal solution to alcohol problems, has been seen as an entirely negative experience, and those interested in alcohol problems and in helping alcoholics have often been concerned to disassociate themselves from the taint of temperance. [20]

Just as the Harrison Narcotics Act turned drug use into a crime, the Volstead Act turned drinking into a crime and created an "industry" for the underworld. While there is some evidence that it decreased alcohol-related problems among the "working class," it created bootlegging, racketeering and related crimes as well as hypocrisy, a breakdown in government machinery and a demoralization of private and public life.[21]

EARLY TREATMENT

The United States has come a long way since the Harrison and Volstead Acts. While we continue our attempts to control drug and alcohol use through legislation, we also try to control it through education and treatment. There had been many voluntary efforts to address the problem of alcoholism, but the greatest success came when William Griffith Wilson (Bill W.) and Dr. Robert Holbrook Smith (Dr. Bob) co-founded Alcoholics Anonymous (AA) in 1935. This was a pivotal point in treatment history that paved the way for many self-help groups to follow. Narcotics Anonymous and Cocaine Anonymous are two offshoots of that extremely successful organization. Al-Anon and Nar-Anon, twelve-step programs for family members and friends, also emerged out of self-help movements. Drug-free therapeutic communities (TCs) got their start indirectly through AA. In 1958 Charles E. Dederich, a former AA member, established Synanon in California as a drug-free treatment center for drug addicts. This was an innovative approach utilizing a powerful encounter component to treat the hardcore drug addict. Other therapeutic communities that followed including Daytop, Phoenix House, Odyssey House, and Project R.E.T.U.R.N. were also structured on the Synanon model. They have since modified their treatment approach to meet the needs of the changing drug culture.

Today there are a vast variety of treatment programs providing a wide range of services. Halfway houses, rehabilitation centers, outpatient clinics, and detoxification programs are located throughout the United States to meet the individual treatment needs of the chemically dependent person. Structured programs of recovery providing individual counseling, group therapy, and education are complementing the efforts of twelve-step fellowship programs. Treatment programs are engaging families in the treatment process and self-help groups are providing help for spouses, children and the loved ones of chemical-dependent persons.

Treatment for the chemical-dependent person has become a business (see Chapter 9). The private sector has joined the voluntary and public sectors in providing services. There are thousands of in-patient residential rehabilitation facilities and outpatient programs throughout the country specializing in alcoholism, other chemical dependencies, and treatment for the mentally impaired chemically addicted (MICA) patient. Families have become very much a part of the treatment process and continuing care is a must if successful outcomes are to be expected.

The rising cost of treatment and the corporate response to contain costs through managed health care has created a competitive environment. While the jury is still out on the long-term impact of managed health care, treatment services providers are competing for business on several levels. The most successful programs are not just delivering good treatment, they are also providing good service and competitive costs.

Good treatment, good service, and competitive costs notwithstanding, the so-called war on drugs will come to a close only when we coordinate our efforts and approach the problem from a public-health perspective. Treatment is one piece of this effort; education and legislation, including law enforcement are the other two. We must examine the role of the host (the user), the agent (the substance), and the environment. Legislation such as the Drug-Free Workplace Act, testing for drug use in certain situations, and containing the supply side are important controls. These measures also serve to create a no-nonsense environment that underscores the seriousness of the problem. Education and prevention, however, will make the difference between containing or reducing the problem. "Secondary prevention," a term once used to identify early intervention, remains an important concept in our efforts to create a drug-free workplace environment. Identifying the troubled employee through job performance is an early intervention strategy. The employee assistance program is a cost-effective system designed to implement this strategy.

NOTES

1. "Seventh Special Report to the U.S. Congress on Alcohol and Health," U.S. Department of Health and Human Services, National Institute on Alcohol Abuse and Alcoholism (1990).

2. Mobil Oil Corporation, "Alcohol & Drug Abuse Program Manual," 1978, 1. Offset.

3. National Institute on Drug Abuse, "National Household Survey on Drug Abuse: Population Estimates 1988," U.S. Department of Health and Human Services (Rockville, MD: 1989), 17.

4. NIDA Capsules. "Research on Drugs in the Workplace," National Institute on Drug Abuse," U.S. Department of Health and Human Services (Rockville, MD: June 1990), 1.

5. Mobil, 1.

6. *The Merck Manual* (Rahway, N.J.: Merck, 1987), 1479.

7. The National Council on Alcoholism and Drug Dependence (NCADD) and the American Society of Addiction Medicine (ASAM), 28th Annual NCADD Conference, Phoenix, AZ, April 26, 1990.

8. *The Merck Manual*, 1476.

9. National Institute on Drug Abuse, "Let's Talk About Drug Abuse" 1979, 10, 3.

10. American Medical Association, "Landmark AMA Policies: Drug Dependencies as Diseases," Resolution 113–Adopted, AMA House of Delegates, June 21–25, 1987.

11. Alcoholism, like diabetes, has no cure. Thus, "I *am* a diabetic," and "I *am* an alcoholic." The term "recovering" rather than "recovered," therefore, is preferred to describe an alcoholic who no longer drinks nor uses mood altering chemicals. This applies no matter how long the person is alcohol and drug free.

12. Harry Milt, *The Revised Basic Handbook on Alcoholism* (Maplewood, NJ: Scientific Aids, 1977), 22.

13. Sheila B. Blume, "Group Psychotherapy in the Treatment of Alcoholism," in *Practical Approaches to Alcoholism Psychotherapy*, eds. Sheldon Zimberg, John Wallace and Sheila B. Blume (New York: Plenum Press, 1978), 70.

14. Andrew Weil, *The Natural Mind* (Boston: Houghton Mifflin, 1973), 17.

15. Edward M. Brecher et al., *Licit & Illicit Drugs: The Consumer Union Report* (Boston: Little Brown, 1972), 3–7.

16. Ibid., 47–55, 115.

17. David Solomon, "The Marijuana Problem in the City of New York," *The Marijuana Papers* (New York: Bobbs-Merrill, 1966), 246.

18. Brecher, 410.

19. Ibid., 51.

20. Mark H. Moore and Dean R. Gerstein, *Alcohol and Public Policy: Beyond the Shadow of Prohibition* (Washington, DC: National Press, 1981), 63.

21. Ibid., 62.

3

The Employer Response to Chemical Dependency: A Historical View

BASIC EAP TERMINOLOGY

Employee assistance program (EAP) is a generic term used to identify any service that addresses the personal problems of an employee. It is sometimes described as an employer-sponsored benefit consisting of diagnostic and referral services for employees and their families. Within any given organization this service may have any of various names. It might be called the Employee Counseling Service, the Personal Assistance Program, the Personal Counseling Service, the Occupational Chemical-Dependency Program, the Special Medical Services Unit, or something else. Major corporations often have EAPs staffed with professionals who handle a range of personal problems while smaller EAPs are more limited in the services they provide. EAP consultants or contractors develop external EAPs for organizations without internal programs. (See Chapter 17 for more on external EAPs.) Some companies have both internal and external programs. Large or small, internal or external, all EAPs are likely to provide assessment and referral services, and use community resources for treatment, counseling, and testing when indicated. As discussed later in this chapter, the EAP evolved out of the occupational alcoholism program (OAP) concept and some programs continue to provide services primarily for alcohol and/or drug-dependent employees. While most EAPs are now "broad brush," providing a wide range of services for troubled employees, the term "troubled employee" as used throughout this book applies to a chemically dependent employee. The term "employee assistance program," unless stated otherwise, is any EAP that addresses this problem. The discussion of services provided for those employees whose job performance is affected by personal problems other than chemical dependency is not within the scope of this book. A brief outline of these services is provided, however, to show the range and the focus that some organizations assume in the design of their programs.

BEYOND EAP SERVICES

While an EAP by definition addresses the problems of employees and their families, a survey of programs across the country shows that some EAPs do more. Many, in fact, could be called "wellness programs" in that the emphasis is on health promotion rather than problem solving. A sampling of services offered includes problem assessment and diagnosis, in-house counseling for both employee and family members, psychiatric evaluations, family therapy, career counseling, financial guidance, legal advice, social activities, housing referral services, chemical-dependency treatment and/or referral for treatment, and employee education and training on a variety of health-care topics. Other programs do only problem assessment and refer the employee to an outside provider service for assistance. Most programs, however, fall somewhere in between.

EAP OBJECTIVES AND GOALS

Whatever services a program offers above and beyond helping employees to solve problems affecting job performance, the EAP's primary objective should not be compromised. That objective is the effectuation of the organization's policies and procedures on identifying and providing assistance for troubled employees. While the objective is to provide assistance, the goal is to keep the good employee working and free of problems that could affect job satisfaction and performance. Neither the range of services offered nor the program's level of sophistication should interfere with this mandate. The New York Business Group on Health (NYBGH), in fact, describes employee counseling programs as "company policies, procedures and services which identify or respond to employees whose personal, emotional or behavioral problems interfere directly or indirectly with work performance." In a handbook published by NYBGH, EAPs can have one of three orientations: single-focus, multiple-focus, or comprehensive.[1] At one end of the continuum would be the single-focus providing only one service, which could be either information/referral or short-term counseling for alcohol and/or drug abusers. Although it could, conceivably, concentrate its efforts on any one employee problem, such as gambling or overeating, its focus is almost always on alcohol abuse and, more recently, chemical dependency. At the opposite extreme would be a comprehensive program offering a range of services provided by a staff of specialists. The scope and size of the program separates it from the multiple-focus program, which may have only one staff member. The multiple-focus program will always include alcohol and/or drug abuse services, but it may compromise its potential effectiveness in attempting to do too much with too little.

EAP DEFINED

Employee assistance programs offer confidential help to employees at all levels of the organization.[2] The National Council on Alcoholism and Drug Dependence (NCADD) defines any such service simply as "A mechanism for implementing an organization's policy on alcoholism and drug abuse." NCADD goes on to say that the organization's position is set forth in the written statement of policy, and the policy is implemented through written procedures.[3] The New York State Division of Substance Abuse Services (DSAS) offers still another description of an EAP. DSAS identifies it as a "unit within a worksetting focused on reaching out to employees with problems, identifying the problem, and assisting in putting that employee in contact with those who can help."[4] The New York State Division of Alcoholism and Alcohol Abuse (DAAA) describes EAPs as programs that "operate as an integral part of an organization to assist employees with problems that can interfere with their ability to function on the job effectively, efficiently, and safely."[5] National and state agencies across the country have similar definitions.

The EAP is, essentially, a confidential, cost-effective, early intervention system designed to help troubled employees with problems that interfere with their ability to function on the job. Deteriorating job performance is usually the basis for referring an employee to an EAP. It is then the function of the EAP practitioner to determine what the underlying problem may be. While the majority of referrals turn out to be alcoholism or drug abuse cases, other personal problems can also affect an employee's functioning. Family problems, depression, gambling, or compulsive eating behaviors are examples of some such problems manifesting symptoms that may resemble chemical dependency. In organizations that have single-focus rather than comprehensive EAPs, however, the cause of the deteriorating job performance is usually determined *before* the referral is made. If the supervisor refers an employee directly to an occupational alcoholism program (OAP), for example, alcohol abuse has already been established. Such a referral is likely to occur only when the employee has a known history of alcoholism or when a company rule has been violated, such as by drinking on the job. The limitation of this model is that it precludes early identification of the chemically dependent person. If the employee is drinking or using drugs on the job, the problem has already progressed beyond the early stages. Some organizations with single-focus EAPs circumvent this problem, however, by requiring that supervisors stick to job performance and refer troubled employees to the medical department for an evaluation rather than to the OAP. Such arrangements work where the OAP is an integral function of the medical department but, more often than not, many such referrals fall through the cracks. This is why "broad-brush" programs—programs that deal with all employee personal problems—are the models that work best. Not only does this model keep the supervisor out of the treatment business, but it allows the employee to participate in an "assistance program" rather than an "alcoholism/drug abuse program." This is particularly important when the program's physical location does not guarantee total privacy.

THE EARLIER INFLUENCES

The industrial movement to drive drinking from the workplace had actually begun before the turn of the century. *The Outlook,* a publication of that period, printed a "succinct account of how sixty-three large firms in the Midwest had discovered that alcohol in almost any quantities [sic] damaged efficiency." The firms' position on drinking in the workplace was that they "used all manner of ways, including discharge, to discourage the use of alcohol."

By the early 1900s, many other employers had taken direct action on the serious drinking problem in the workplace. The steel industry had begun dismissing employees for drinking on the job and many American railroads required total abstinence—both on and off the job.[6]

The Temperance Movement, Taylorism, and Workmen's Compensation were the earlier motivating forces behind industries' efforts to rid the workplace of alcohol. The moralistically desirable personal characteristics of discipline, self-reliance, and hard work; the new scientific concept of commercial efficiency; and the fact that the employer would be held financially responsible for injuries incurred

by employees on the job were the major societal/industrial influences.[7]

In spite of these influences, alcohol and alcoholism were not
eliminated from the workplace. After a period of reduced consumption, drinking increased and efficiency became a serious concern, once
again, as the United States prepared for World War II. Three potent
forces soon combined, however, providing industry with new incentives to deal with this growing concern:

First was the birth and rapid growth of Alcoholics Anonymous
(AA). Second, influential and dedicated medical directors came to
support and actively initiate programs during this period, providing
a high status leadership to the emerging programs. Third, the unique
labor market conditions during World War II, that is, that there was a
desparate need of manpower.[8]

THE EARLY PROGRAMS

The EAP concept practiced today has its roots in the earlier occupational alcoholism program (OAP) model of the 1940s. The evolution
of the concept from helping employees with drinking problems to
helping employees with *any* personal problems picked up momentum
in 1965 when a study by the NCADD indicated that programs should
focus on job performance rather than on alcoholism symptoms for the
purpose of early identification of alcoholic employees.[9] Prior to that
time supervisors were expected to watch for behavioral, physical, and
social indications of alcohol abuse. They were "trained" to note
cutaneous symptoms such as a red nose, to watch for staggering
employees, and for employees with alcohol on the breath.

As stated in Chapter 2, this approach to identifying troubled
employees would reveal just the tip of the iceberg. The change to a
focus on job performance was important in that it served to identify
troubled employees early on, often before they began drinking or
drugging on the job. But equally important is that this change required
the supervisor to function only as a supervisor and not as a diagnos-
tician. Deteriorating job performance, often an early sign of alcoholism or drug abuse, would now be the supervisor's concern—
looking for "drunks" would not.

Troubled employees who are identified through this method are
then referred to the employee assistance program where an assessment is made, and treatment, if indicated, is planned. While most
referrals to the EAP would prove to be alcohol problems, many, as
discussed in the previous section, would be employees with other
personal problems, hence the beginning of the "broad-brush" concept

of troubled employee identification. When the first formal multi-plant OAPs were launched in the early 1940s alcoholism was the only concern. While it is difficult to credit any one company with the first OAP, Trice and Schonbrunn name E.I. DuPont de Nemours and Company and the Eastman Kodak Corporation on the East Coast, and North American Aviation on the West Coast as "having the basic elements of a program" at that time.[10]

Many people and events are recorded that influenced early program development, but one event in particular between two key personalities is of special significance. That is a meeting between Maurice DuPont Lee, Chairman of E.I. DuPont de Nemours and William Griffith Wilson (Bill W.), cofounder of Alcoholics Anonymous.[11] It is suspected that AA's success in helping alcoholics since its beginnings in 1935, and Mr. Lee's need to deal with the problem in the workplace, were discussed, and perhaps the idea for an occupational program was fueled.

One report by the National Institute on Alcohol Abuse and Alcoholism credits E.I. DuPont with the first known multi-plant program and Eastman Kodak with the second, both in 1944.[12] Whichever came first, many other organizations, large and small, followed. They included North American Aviation, the Hudson Department Store, the Western Electric Company, the Caterpillar Tractor Company, Thompson Aircraft Products, and the United States Navy.[13] New York Life Insurance Company, Allis Chalmers, and Consolidated Edison later joined the growing number of companies offering help to the alcoholic employee.

TWENTY THOUSAND EAPs NOW IN PLACE

The concept of occupational alcoholism programming had, obviously, taken hold. By 1959 there were fifty major companies with programs in place and by 1973 there were five hundred programs nationwide.[14] There are presently some twenty thousand programs operating in the United States.[15] These programs can be found in virtually every type of organization where people are employed. Local police and fire departments have programs as do airlines, railroads, manufacturing firms, labor unions, sports associations, municipalities, service organizations, and advertising agencies. Smaller companies often group together and form consortiums and others enter into contractual arrangements with EAP consulting firms. Work organizations in the public, private and voluntary sectors have discovered that EAPs are a very effective approach, and often a very efficient approach, to reducing alcoholism and drug abuse.

The Employee Assistancs Professionals Association (formerly AL-MACA) predicted in 1984 that every employed person in the country would be covered by an employee assistance program by 1990.[16] While this prediction proved to be overly optimistic, 86.8 percent of all employees who work in organizations with five thousand or more employees are now covered. That figure drops significantly, however, when smaller organizations are added. Only 31 percent of all organization surveyed had EAPs.[17] A study by the New York State Department of Labor shows an even greater discrepancy between large and small organizations. Seventy percent of those organizations with two thousand or more employees are providing EAP services, while only 12 percent with 750 to 2,000 employees have EAPs.[18] These data tell us that a large portion of the employee population is not yet covered by EAPs, yet leaders in business and industry recognize the importance of providing such services. The need for employee assistance programming in small- to medium-size organizations continues to exist. This provides an opportunity for external EAP contractors.

THE EVENTS THAT PAVED THE WAY

The concept of employee assistance has evolved and grown over the last five decades. A look at relevant events and activities since those early days of occupational alcoholism programming supports this fact:

1944. Dupont establishes the first known alcoholism program in a major multi-plant company.

1944. National Council on Alcoholism (NCA) now called the National Council on Alcoholism and Drug Dependence (NCADD) established.

1944. Eastman Kodak establishes the second major multi-plant company program, handled through its medical department, with emphasis on Alcoholics Anonymous approach to recovery.

1947. International Doctors' group in AA established.

1956. American Medical Association resolves that alcoholism is a disease.

1959. NCA estimates that 50 companies have formal programs in full operation. The stereotype of the alcoholic person beyond help remains a deterrent to new program initiatives.

1960. NCA Industrial Committee established (later called Labor-Management Committee).

1965. NCA study indicates programs should place focus on job performance for the purpose of early identification of alcoholic employees.

1969. NCA's Labor-Management Committee established.

1970. Enactment of the Hughes Act establishes NIAAA-funded state programs.

1971. United Auto Workers International Executive Board adopts policy statement for joint union-management alcohol programs.

1971. Association of Labor-Management Administrators and Consultants on Alcoholism, Inc. (ALMACA), now called the Employee Assistance Professionals Association, Inc., formed.

1972. First Federal Aviation Administration exemption for alcoholism granted to air transport pilots.

1972. NIAAA offers staffing grants to support the work of two Occupational Program Consultants (OPCs)in each state.

1973. Approximately 500 occupational alcoholism programs in operation nationwide.

1974. Seventy-five percent of Blue Cross plans (62 percent of Blue Shield) have some type of alcoholism coverage available.

1974. Air Line Pilots Association Human Intervention and Motivation Study (HIMS) begins operation.

1975. International Lawyers in AA group established.

1976. University of Missouri established employee assistance program for facility and staff.

1977. 2,400 employee alcoholism programs are at some stage of development in public and private employment centers in all 50 states.[19]

And in more recent times:

1980. Baseball major leagues implement employee assistance programs.

1982. National Football League (NFL) enters into agreement with the Hazelden Foundation to provide EAP services for chemical-dependent players.[20]

1983. Several states pass legislation mandating insurance companies to offer coverage for alcoholism/drug abuse treatment.

1984. National Basketball Association (NBA) enters into contract with Control Data Corporation's Life Extension Institute to provide EAP for chemical dependent players.[21]

1984. 8,000 employee assistance programs addressing alcohol, drug, and other troubled employee problems are in place and operating.[22]

1985. ALMACA hires credentialing specialist in first step of process to build database and develop criteria for credentialing employee assistance professionals.[23]

1986. Colleges and universities develop curriculum offering graduate degrees and/or certificates in employee assistance.

1987. The American Medical Association resolves that all drug dependencies, including alcoholism, are diseases.

1987. On May 16, the first certification examination for employee assistance professionals (CEAP) is given.

1988. The Drug Free Workplace Act of 1988 is enacted.

1989. A pivotal study conducted by Alexander & Alexander on McDonnell Douglas employees reinforces cost benefit of employee assistance programs.

1989. The Association of Labor-Management Administrators and Consultants on Alcoholism, Inc. (ALMACA), changes its name to the Employee Assistance Professionals Association, Inc. (EAP Association).

1990. New York State Assembly EAP Task Force agrees to proposed legislation on managed health care operations, EAPs in law enforcement, and EAPs for addiction service providers.

1990. Society of Americans for Recovery (SOAR) founded by Former U.S. Senator Harold E. Hughes.

1991. More than 20,000 employee assistance programs addressing alcohol, drug, and other troubled employee problems are in place and operating.[24]

THE CHANGES AND THE CHALLENGES

Organizations that have employee assistance programs know that their investment will continue to yield returns in one form or another. These returns may be expressed in both quantitative and non-quantitative terms, a subject to be discussed fully in later chapters. It would suffice to say here, therefore, that most organizations with EAPs in place can show that such programs reduce both the cost of alcohol and drug-related problems, and the human suffering associated with such problems. When one considers the successful alcoholism recovery rate of employees referred to EAPs— some organizations claim as high as 75 percent—the value of the EAP is evident. Many employees who probably would have eventually lost their jobs, their families, and perhaps their lives have been provided an opportunity to seek treatment and become productive employees once again. Since the population the EAP benefits is within the organization, it follows that the organization ultimately benefits.[25]

The challenge for work organizations and for employee assistance programs does not lie, however, in the success they already know. The growth of the EAP movement since those first programs were implemented in the 1940s is evidence that the concept has been successful.

This success and the value of having an EAP is not likely to change. The primary challenge lies in the changing employee population. While alcohol will continue to be America's number one problem, the troubled employee of the nineties uses and abuses many different drugs, including alcohol. Unlike the troubled employee of the past, this person is more likely to be chemically dependent than a person who only drinks too much. The values of this individual will also be different—sometimes only slightly, but different. "He" is as likely to be a "she." Words like "line," "ice," "gram," "joint," and "straight" will be heard as often as "booze," "drunk," "faced," and "sober." Even the drinking habits in America are changing. "Bourbon and soda" and "scotch and water" have been replaced by more fashionable concoctions with trendy names.

Work organizations can no longer ignore the problem of drugs in the workplace. Those without drug and alcohol policies must now face the seriousness of the problem. Controversy around drug testing, the Drug-Free Workplace Act, and managed health care are calling attention to this fact. For organizations with programs in place, ethical and legal dilemmas around such issues are an ongoing concern. Professional standards, those that govern the practice of employee assistance programming, are more necessary now than ever.

Federal and state anti-discrimination and confidentiality laws and regulations remain an important consideration. Employers are often correct in assuming that these laws do not apply to them; that only outside treatment programs providing alcohol or drug diagnoses, treatment, or referral for treatment must concern themselves with such issues. EAPs are not treatment programs and, except for those organizations that receive federal funding, are likely to be exempt from federal rules. Nevertheless, as will be discussed in Chapter 16, legal council should be sought concerning federal and local compliance.

Another important consideration for all work organizations, those with and without EAPs, is the growing concern of skyrocketing health-care costs. Alcoholism and drug abuse, if left untreated, will inevitably result in illness and injury requiring hospitalization. The cost of such hospitalizations is ultimately paid for by the employer through high insurance premiums and disability claims. It is a cost that the organizations without EAPs will have little control over. Organizations with programs, however, are in a better position to monitor such costs. (As will be discussed in Chapters 6 and 7, a recent financial impact study on McDonnell Douglas Corporation employees shows a 4:1 return on investment.) First, they can identify the chemical-dependent person at an early stage, often before the problem causes serious medical complications requiring hospitalization.

Second, the organization can mandate that employees seeking treatment specifically for alcoholism or drug abuse come through the EAP. The EAP would assess the employee's treatment needs and make an appropriate referral to a preferred (based on quality care and cost) treatment provider. Some benefit plans encourage EAP utilization by providing higher reimbursement rates for employees referred to treatment by the EAP. The employee who submits a claim for detoxification and rehabilitation, for example, will receive 80 percent if referred by the EAP but only 50 percent if not. Most managed health care and utilization management plans, in fact, require precertification for admission. The EAP can be an effective gatekeeper in determining the appropriate level of care necessary and the cost for such services.

Another important consideration is offering the services of the EAP to retired employees. Alcoholism is a growing problem among the elderly, and the risk of serious related health problems is even greater in this group. Most retirees are covered by the insurance policy of their last employer and the cost of treatment is paid through higher premiums. Where the organization is self-insured, this cost is even more evident. The availability of an EAP for this group is likely to reduce this cost, and equally important, provide a familiar and friendly resource for the retiree.

The corporate response to alcohol and drug related problems has intensified over the past several years. The Drug-Free Workplace Act of 1988 has, in part, prompted a closer look at such issues. Provisions of this act, while applicable only to employers receiving federal funds, are being followed by many organizations not required by law to comply.

The controversy around drug testing has also been a factor in prompting business and industry to look at itself. While most work organizations do not test employees for drug use, the issue has raised consciousness about the problem. Railway accidents, drugs in professional sports, and the successful recovery of high-profile personalities have all contributed to the present awareness about drug use and recovery. As leaders in business and industry become more aware of the impact of drugs and alcohol on productivity, profit, and safety, the search for effective solutions continues. The EAP, because it focuses on job performance and productivity, remains the most logical strategy in any effort to establish a drug-free work environment.

NOTES

1. Howard V. Schmitz, *The Handbook of Employee Counseling Programs* (New York: The New York Business Group on Health, 1982), 15.

2. Ibid., 26–31.

3. William S. Duncan, *The EAP Manual* (New York: National Council on Alcoholism), 20.

4. "Employee Assistance Programs: Training Needs and Resources," July 1984, 1 (mimeographed).

5. "DAAA Guidelines For Development of Alcoholism and Alcohol Abuse Guidelines," June 1990, 4 (mimeographed).

6. Harrison M. Trice and Mona Schonbrunn, "A History of Job-based Alcoholism Programs: 1900–1955," *Journal of Drug Issues*, (ILR Reprint, Cornell University) Spring 1981: 178.

7. Ibid., 173.

8. Ibid., 175.

9. National Institute on Alcohol Abuse and Alcoholism (NIAAA), "Target: Alcohol Abuse in the Hard-To-Reach Work Force" 1982, 3.

10. Trice and Schonbrunn, "A History," 174.

11. Walter Scanlon, "Trends in EAPs: Then and Now," *EAP Digest* (May/June 1983): 38–41.

12. NIAAA, "Target," 2.

13. Trice and Schonbrunn, "A History," 176.

14. NIAAA, "Target," 6.

15. Association of Employee Assistance Professionals Association, "EAP Standards," Arlington, VA, April 16, 1990 (draft).

16. Betty Ready, "ALMACA's Membership Problem," *The ALMACAN* 14, Issue 4 (April 1984): 4.

17. Bureau of Labor Statistics, *The World Almanac 1990* (New York: Pharos Books, 1990), 105.

18. New York State Department of Labor and The New York State Division of Alcoholism and Alcohol Abuse, "Employeed Population by Work Organization," June 7, 1990.

19. NIAAA, "Target," 2–16.

20. James O'Hare, "EAPs in Professional Sports," *The ALMACAN* 14, Issue 5 (May 1984): 3.

21. Ibid.

22. Reddy, 3.

23. *The ALMACAN* 15, Issue 1 (January 1985): 1.

24. EAP Standards, 1990.

25. Walter Scanlon, "Trends in EAPs: Then and Now," *EAP Digest* (May/June 1983): 38–41.

4

The Government Response: Drug-Free Workplace Legislation

DRUG-FREE WORKPLACE REGULATIONS

The Omnibus Drug Act (ODA), a sweeping anti-drug bill passed by Congress on October 17, 1986, authorized $1.7 billion for enforcement and education programs. This was to be the first of several pieces of legislation that would attempt to address the growing drug-abuse problem in the United States.

On November 18, 1988, in response to the continuing spread of drug abuse, President Reagan signed into law an addition to the ODA named the Anti-Drug Abuse Act of 1988 (Title V, Subtitle D of P.L. 100-690).[1] This act, in its final form, addresses such issues as illegal money laundering, child pornography, obscenity, and drug-free workplace requirements for federal contractors. Dropped from the bill in a compromise between the House and the Senate were such add-ons as AIDS confidentiality guidelines and drug-testing laboratory standards.

The Drug-Free Workplace Act of 1988 (DFWA), a part of The Anti-Drug Abuse Act of 1988, went into effect on March 18, 1989. The final DFWA regulations were published in the Federal Register of May 25, 1990.[2] The Office of Management and Budget (OMB) is the governing agency responsible for publishing the DFWA regulations and implementing its provisions.

It might be important to note here the difference between a *statute* and a *regulation*. With the implementation of new laws such as the Drug-Free Workplace Act, some aspects are enforceable by "statute" and some by "regulation." A statute is the public law itself. In the case of the Drug-Free Workplace Act, the statute is Title V, Subtitle D of P.L. 100-690 (known as the Anti-Drug Abuse Act).

A regulation is that which has been written by a regulatory agency, usually the Office of Management and Budget, which further defines or clarifies the statute. A regulation cannot rewrite the law.[3]

COMPLIANCE WITH THE DRUG-FREE WORKPLACE ACT

For the most part, the Drug-Free Workplace Act does not apply to private industry and business. It requires both federal contractors receiving more than $25,000 and federal grantees to certify that they will provide a drug-free workplace. This is a condition of their contract and/or grant. And even those organizations receiving federal monies may not necessarily have to comply under the regulations as written.

The regulations define "grant," for example, as block grants and entitlement programs. This means that the grant must come directly from a federal agency to a grantee. For example, if an organization receives block grant assistance through a state agency, the state agency, but not the organization, is covered by the act. If the organization also receives direct federal funding, however, it *is* covered by the act. Receiving Medicaid funds does not bring an organization under coverage of the act.

The regulations define "contract" to include contracts from *any* federal agency. Programs that receive contracts equal to or in excess of $25,000 are covered under the regulations. Individuals who receive a contract of any amount must also comply with the regulations.

DEFINING THE DRUG-FREE WORKPLACE

A drug-free workplace is defined under the new regulations as a worksite at which employees of the grantee or contractor are prohibited from engaging in the unlawful manufacture, distribution, dispensing, possession, or use of a controlled substance. Criminal activities that occur off the worksite are not covered under the statute or regulations.

The first question one might ask about the drug-free workplace as defined under the new regulations is whether or not such legislation is really necessary. After all, no work organization would tolerate drug use on the worksite. A cocaine-using employee who comes to the attention of management would almost certainly be disciplined. As for selling or manufacturing controlled substances, termination is, at the very least, the action that would be taken. While most work organizations are not likely to call outside attention to the problem, some may have existing policies that call for law enforcement involvement.

As discussed above, the Office of Management and Budget is responsible for writing the regulations and implementing the Drug-Free Workplace Act of 1988. In order to comply with the act, covered grantees and contractors (not individuals) must:

1. Certify that they will maintain a drug-free workplace (as described above).
2. Inform employees that they cannot engage in unlawful drug-related activities on the worksite and specify actions that will be taken against employees who violate that prohibition.
3. Establish a drug-free awareness program to inform employees about the dangers of drug abuse in the workplace, the penalties for violations at the worksite, and the availability of drug counseling and rehabilitation programs.
4. Notify employees that as a condition of employment under the grant or contract, the employee must abide by the drug-free workplace statement and must inform the employer of any criminal conviction for a violation of a drug statute for an incident that occurred at the workplace no later than five days after the conviction.
5. Report any employee's drug-related workplace conviction to the relevant federal grantor/contracting agency within ten days of receiving notice of that conviction.
6. Within thirty days of receiving notice of employee's drug-related workplace conviction, take appropriate personnel action against the employee (up to and including termination) or require the employee to participate satisfactorily in a drug-abuse rehabilitation or assistance program; and
7. Make a good faith effort to continue to maintain a drug-free workplace by implementing the activities above.[4]

While the above summary is based on the interim regulations written by the OMB in March 1989, the final regulations offer little change. It is noteworthy that the OMB has identified components that could, but need not, be included in a drug-free workplace program. Those components include employee education, employee assistance, supervisory training, and drug detection through drug testing and increased security. The OMB's deliberate reference to these components is open to interpretation. If a grantee adds all the components to its drug-free workplace program, however, it will have a better program than if it added none.[5]

CLARIFICATION AND COMPLIANCE WITH THE ACT

Compliance with the act appears to be straightforward and enforceable. Yet a closer look reveals gray areas that need interpretation.

A grantee or contractor might be concerned about his role in the law enforcement process leading to a criminal conviction of an employee. If it comes to the attention of the employer that a particular employee is engaged in illegal activities as defined, is it the employer's responsibility to alert law enforcement? Or if drug use is rampant at the worksite, is it the employer's responsibility to conduct investigative work in an effort to make a case against violators?

Item 2, above, requires the employer to "take action against employees who violate that prohibition." The "prohibition" would be a drug-free workplace as defined in item 1. This may mean that it is the employer's responsibility to confront the situation or individual(s) and warn them of the consequences of such activity while offering assistance through counseling and rehabilitation programs.

Yet items 4, 5, and 6 focus on "criminal conviction" and require the employer to "report any employee's drug-related workplace conviction to the relevant federal grantor or contracting agency."

As for item 3, implementation of the Drug-Free Workplace Act could involve costs that may not have been budgeted for. Establishing a drug-free awareness program replete with drug counseling and rehabilitation programs could be costly and time consuming. And is it financially and/or practically feasible for an individual contractor to establish a drug-free awareness program?

While attempting to understand the statute and how best to be in compliance with its requirements may present problems of clarification, the key to compliance lies in item 7 and the qualifier "good faith effort."

In terms of establishing a drug-free awareness program to inform employees about the dangers of drug abuse in the workplace, the costs for this program are considered allowable under the grant. In applying for a grant, the grantee should detail the program, its implementation, and cost in the proposal. As for individual contractors and grantees, they must certify that they will comply with the regulations, but do not have to establish a drug-free awareness program.

VIOLATION OF THE ACT

The Legal Action Center says that a violation of the act and regulations constitutes any one of the following:

1. The grantee or contractor submits a false certification.
2. The grantee or contractor fails to comply with the certification or
3. A substantial number of employees are convicted of violations of criminal drug statutes stemming from incidents that occurred on the worksite, indicating that the employer has failed to make a good faith effort to provide a drug-free workplace.

A "good faith effort" is a vague and nebulous qualifier that leaves plenty of room for arguments both pro and con compliance and violation. It is the kind of condition used when there is little clearcut understanding of what will constitute a violation. The specifics of a "good faith effort" are to be determined for years to come by the Office of Management and Budget, the administrative judges who will rule on alleged violations, and even the federal courts responsible for interpreting the law and setting precedents.

THE SANCTIONS AND WAVERS

The most logical penalty for violators of the Drug-Free Workplace Act is financial. The regulations permit the granting or contracting agency to take one of three actions in the event of violations. They are as follows:

1. The agency can suspend or withhold payments under the contract.
2. The agency can terminate the grant or contract.
3. The agency can debar the grantee or contractor for a period of up to five years.

The agency has complete discretion in determining the sanction, but the agency head can waive the sanction if he or she finds that a waiver is in the public interest.

The agency must also determine the appropriate unit within an organization to sanction. The commentary to the regulations indicates that generally only the department, unit, or division responsible for performing the grant or contract should be subject to the sanction. Thus, for example, if several different units within an agency perform work under many grants or contracts, but only one of the units violates a requirement of the regulations, only that unit should be subject to sanctions. The other units of the agency should not be affected. If on the other hand, an entire organization is considered responsible for the implementation of a grant or contract, the entire organization could be subject to sanctions.[6]

This is another gray area that will be settled on a case-by-case basis. Assuming that a grantee or a contractor with several worksites is in violation of DFWA regulations, it would have to be determined whether the organization or one of its units is in violation. One way to minimize the possibility of this becoming an issue is to have the grantee or contractor declare how it intends to implement its program(s). How the organization intends to comply with the act would be included in the grant application or contract proposal.

THE DRUG-FREE WORKPLACE ACT OF 1988 VERSUS THE FEDERAL REHABILITATION ACT OF 1973

The Legal Action Center, in contemplating the question whether or not compliance with the DFWA violates the Federal Rehabilitation Act provisions, offers the following discussion:

The short answer is no, it will not. The Federal Rehabilitation Act prohibits discrimination against individuals with handicaps who are otherwise qualified for the job. The Act applies to substance abusers unless "current use of alcohol or drugs prevents [them] from performing the duties of the job in question or [unless their] employment, by reason of such current alcohol or drug abuse, would constitute a direct threat to property or the safety of others" (29 U.S.C. & 706(7)(B)).

The Rehabilitation Act does not, however, prohibit an employer from promulgating rules prohibiting the possession, use, or distribution of drugs at the workplace or from enforcing those rules with disciplinary action, so long as the rules are applied uniformly to drug abuser and non-drug abuser alike.

Thus, an employer subject to both the Drug-Free Workplace Act of 1988 and the Rehabilitation Act of 1973 should establish a policy prohibiting the use, possession or distribution of drugs at the workplace, notify employees of that policy (including the consequences of violations of the policy), enforce the policy in a non-discriminatory fashion, and follow the other requirements of the Drug-Free Workplace Act listed above.[7]

LABOR UNIONS AND THE DRUG-FREE WORKPLACE ACT

Labor unions may have two good reasons to study the Drug-Free Workplace Act and fully understand its regulations. First, a labor union may be the recipient of a federal grant or contract with a federal agency qualifying it as a covered employer. Second, it must fully understand DFWA requirements in order to insure that its membership is not victimized in the name of the act. In the words of John J. Sweeney, president of the Service Employees International Union, AFL-CIO, "It is very important that you know exactly what this new law requires and who it covers, in order to prevent employers from overreaching its requirements."[8]

DRUG TESTING AND THE DRUG-FREE WORKPLACE ACT

The Drug-Free Workplace Act does not require that grantees or contractors use toxicology to comply with the regulations. The decision to use drug testing in an effort to deal with the problem is a decision reached outside the requirements prepared by the Office of Management and Budget. OMB has coordinated regulatory development with over thirty federal agencies to ensure uniform government-wide implementation of this act. OMB issued a notice providing information, in the form of nonbinding questions and answers, to assist the public in meeting the requirements of the act. Question number ten is:

Do either the Drug-Free Workplace Act or its implementing regulations published today (January 31, 1989) require contractors or grantees to conduct drug tests of employees? The answer: No.[9]

THE DEPARTMENTS OF TRANSPORTATION AND DEFENSE

While the Drug-Free Workplace Act does not require drug testing to be in compliance, two major federal agencies, The Department of Transportation (DOT) and the Department of Defense (DOD), do have drug-testing provisions.

The DOT, under the "Mandatory Guidelines for Federal Workplace Drug Testing Programs" of the Department of Health and Human Services, issued regulations requiring anti-drug programs in the aviation motor carrier, railroad, maritime, mass transit, and pipeline industries to conduct drug testing (Federal Register, Department of

Transportation Requirements, November 21, 1988). The requirement for all of its agencies to establish drug-testing programs can be linked directly to a well-publicized crash in 1987 of two trains in Chase, Maryland, in which the engineer at fault tested positive for marijuana.[10] The department's operating administrations (Federal Aviation Administration, Federal Highway Administration, Federal Railroad Administration, United States Coast Guard, Urban Mass Transportation Administration, and Research and Special Programs Administration) are covered under this rule (49 CFR Part 40, et al).[11]

The DOD, under 48 CFR Parts 223 and 252, requires that

The Contractor shall establish a program that provides for testing for the use of illegal drugs by employees in sensitive positions. The extent of and criteria for such testing shall be determined by the Contractor based on considerations that include the Nature of the work being performed under the contract, the employee's duties, the efficient use of Contractor resources, and the risks to public health, safety, and national security that could result from the failure of an employee adequately to discharge his or her position.

The regulation's criteria for testing include:

1. When there is a reasonable suspicion that an employee uses illegal drugs.
2. When an employee has been involved in an accident or unsafe practice.
3. As part of or as a follow-up to counseling or rehabilitation for illegal drug (Controlled substances included in Schedule I and II, as defined by section 802(6) of Title 21 of the United States Code, the position of which is unlawful under Chapter 13 of that Title).
4. As part of a voluntary employee drug testing program.[12]

The requirements specified by DOD are designed to encourage a flexible approach to dealing with the problem of drug use among employees. Thus, the rule prescribes certain elements that must be included in the covered contractor's drug-free workplace program, but does not specify the details or criteria for implementation. In addition to a program for testing employees for illegal drug use, the DOD regulation provides that a federal contractor's program for achieving a drug-free workplace include an employee assistance program, training for supervisors so they can identify and address illegal drug use by employees, and a provision for self-referrals and supervisory referrals for treatment.[13]

As discussed earlier, there is a difference between a statute and a regulation. The drug-testing policies of both the Department of Transportation and the Department of Defense are not requirements of the Drug-Free Workplace Act and therefore are not required by statute. They are written by DOT and DOD and enforced under the Code of Federal Regulations.

THE DFWA IS JUST THE BEGINNING

This is an important piece of legislation because it opens the door for change. Three new bills have been introduced that focus on treatment, control, and interdiction activities. These include bills by Senator Kennedy, Senator Biden and, for the administration, Senator Dole. The Kennedy bill, *The Drug Abuse Treatment and Prevention Improvement Act of 1990* (S.2649) focuses exclusively on treatment and prevention services and research, while the Biden bill, *The National Drug Control Strategy Act of 1990* (S.2650) addresses the broader range of issues identified in Senator Biden's counter drug strategy. The Administration's bill, the *National Drug Control Strategy Implementation Act of 1990* (S.2652) focuses primarily on supply reduction and interdiction activities.[14] While the provisions of these bills would be too much to detail here, this flurry of legislative activity is an attempt to fill in the holes in the DFWA. If one is to be optimistic, this activity will result in new and effective drug control regulations and policies. Most important, it may bring us closer to a drug-free workplace.

THE ACT SETS STANDARDS FOR ALL
WORK ORGANIZATIONS

The Drug-Free Workplace Act of 1988 and its federal enactments, both present and future, are complex and exacting. It has far reaching implications and responsibilities for those private-sector employers receiving federal grants or under federal contract. Because of these complexities and the severe penalties for violating the act's provisions or not complying with the federal regulations, it is important that employers study the guidelines and take every step necessary to honor them.[15]

Recipients of such funds are expected to comply with regulations, rules, and guidelines that are not yet totally clear. Further complicating the task of interpreting the act and its provisions are the federal rules on drug testing under the Department of Transportation and Department of Defense. These rules add still another dimension to the task of maintaining a drug-free workplace. Yet one could argue that using legislation to maintain a drug-free workplace could prove effective. While it may be impossible to legislate sobriety, such legislation is likely to encourage an environment conducive to drug-free thinking. A drug-free environment has always been good business and now it's the law.

The Drug-Free Workplace Act of 1988 will be embraced by some organizations. In work environments where getting paper clips requires an act of Congress, mandating programs to deal with drug problems is the only way to deal with such problems. It will provide management with the support it needs to get its job done and unions with a set of guidelines with which to evaluate management's actions. Both union and management must understand both the statute and its regulations. While "compliance" is the word most often associated with government regulations, the Drug-Free Workplace Act may actually have some redeeming qualities. For one thing, its provisions include programs aimed at educating the workplace about drug use and counseling employees who are chemically dependent. Employee assistance programs will probably play an important role in complying with this provision. The act also sets standards and offers guidelines that non-covered organizations can use in their efforts to establish drug-free workplaces.

NOTES

1. Legal Action Center, "The Drug-Free Workplace Act," Background Materials (New York: Legal Action Center, 1989).

2. Legal Action Center, "ActionWatch," June 1990.

3. Public Policy, "Drug-Free Workplace Regulations Released," the *ALMACAN* 19, No. 3 (March 1989).

4. Legal, "The Drug-Free Workplace Act," 1989.

5. Legal Action Center, "ActionWatch," June 1990

6. Legal, "The Drug-Free Workplace Act," 1989.

7. Ibid.

8. John J. Sweeney, general announcement, Service Employees International Union, dated March 22, 1989.

9. *Federal Register*, 54, No. 19, Tuesday, January 31, 1989, Notices.

10. "FAA Releases Airline Drug Testing Regs," *The ALMACAN*, 19, No. 3 (March 1989): 15.

11. Portfolio of Information on the 1988 Drug-Free Workplace Act and Federal EAP Regulations (Employee Assistance Program Association, 1989), 16–18.

12. Ibid., 19, 20.

13. Bruce S. Harrison, Esq., and Gary L. Simpler, Esq., "Toward a Drug-Free Workplace: Federal Initiatives," *EAP Digest,* 9 No. 6, (September/October 1989): 19–23.

14. Legal Action Center, "ActionWatch," May 1990.

15. Ibid.

5

EAP Practice and Process

HOW IT WORKS

"Rarely have we seen a person fail who has thoroughly followed our path" are words that could describe the assistance provided through an EAP. Quoted, in fact, from the 1939 book *Alcoholics Anonymous*, these words launched Chapter 5, "How It [Alcoholics Anonymous] Works." Acknowledging that employee assistance programs followed the success of Alcoholics Anonymous, and with respect to the growth of these two somewhat related but separate program models, here are how EAPs work:

There are at least three ways an employee can get to the company EAP: as a self-referral, as a medical referral, or as a supervisory referral. While some EAPs boast a self-referral rate as high as 60 percent, only a small number of these are likely to report chemical dependency as the stated concern. In most organizations employees are referred, directly or indirectly, by supervisors.[1] Even many employees who appear to be self-referred may actually have been prompted to contact the EAP during an informal supervisory confrontation.[2] Nevertheless, some employees do seek out the company employee assistance program on their own and avail themselves of the services offered, a subject fully discussed in Chapter 8.

In terms of the treatment offered to a self-referred employee versus that offered a supervisor-referred employee, there is, of course, no difference. Each will, hopefully, receive the same level and quality of service. The difference is in what happens when the employee refuses to cooperate in treatment or decides to discontinue treatment. If he or she is self-referred, nothing happens. It was the employee who initiated the contact and it is the employee's right to discontinue treatment at will. The program counselor will usually make some effort to re-engage the employee if continued treatment is necessary, but the decision to continue remains the employee's.

An employee referred by the company's medical department may also have the right to refuse treatment if he or she chooses. Unless the employee's condition is affecting job performance, or the employee's behavior jeopardizes personal safety or the safety of others, a medical referral is not likely to be considered a condition of continued employment. The employee reserves the right to accept or refuse help. In this way a medical referral is similar to a self-referral.

The employee who is referred to the EAP by a supervisor, however, has a somewhat different status. The referral may have been made as an alternative to disciplinary action after a warning interview. While this employee also has the right of choice, refusing to accept the referral or not cooperating in treatment may trigger action leading to disciplinary procedures (see Figure 5.1). The warning interview, as used in many work organizations, is a specific management procedure applied when the employee's performance remains unsatisfactory following an earlier intervention interview. This happens regardless of whether or not the employee is currently engaged with the EAP. The warning interview initiates a probationary period during which the employee must achieve a satisfactory level of performance or face the possibility of discharge.[3]

A term used to describe the process by which an employee is encouraged to seek out the services of the company EAP is often referred to as a "constructive confrontation," a term coined by H.M. Trice. He says:

> The decline in job performance that accompanies problem drinking is used as a basis for constructively offering alternative courses of behavior. Such employees should also be given emotional support and practical assistance, designed to direct them toward rehabilitation. Constructive confrontation represents an application of a social learning paradigm that is currently coming into prominence in the field of behavioral sciences.[4]

If the troubled employee is a member of a labor union, a union representative will usually be present during a constructive confrontation. In some cases, in fact, the union representative may be a party to the confrontation process. This is not likely to happen where the EAP is a management program but rather where the EAP is a joint union-management effort, a subject discussed in Chapter 12.

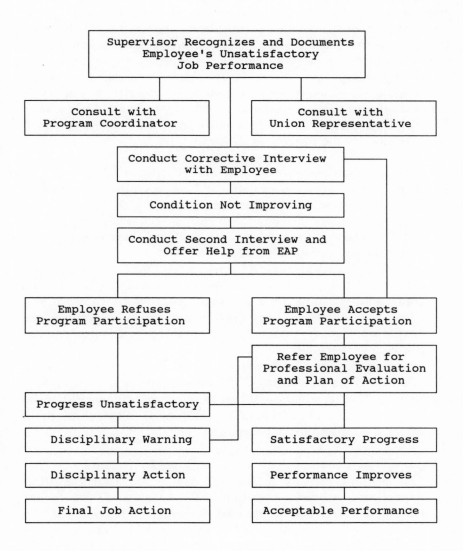

Figure 5.1 Procedural Flow Chart

THE SUPERVISOR'S ROLE

Whether the EAP is a union program, a joint union-management program or a management program, the critical factor to its success is the chemically dependent person's employment. The decline in job performance that accompanies the problem is used, as stated above, "as a basis for constructively offering alternative courses of behavior." The constructive confrontation can be effective, however, only if the supervisor is doing the job he or she is expected to do: supervise. Knowledge about alcoholism, drug abuse, and other personal problems, as discussed in earlier chapters, is not nearly as important as knowledge of the accepted and proven methods for dealing with these problems. There are five generally accepted basic steps which must be taken by the supervisor. These are:

Recognition that a problem exists and that there is a pattern of deteriorating work performance. When presenting the problem to the employee, it is important to describe the performance problem as observed and not to diagnosis or evaluate the personal problem causing the performance problem. This is sometimes called the "observation" stage.

Documentation and keeping an up-to-date file of the employee's work performance is important. Without it, an otherwise effective confrontation can turn into a case of "your word against mine." Also, the employee may actually be unaware that job performance is affected. Having proof helps the employee to comprehend the problem as it actually is.

Action is the progressive formal disciplinary procedure consisting of informal verbal warnings, corrective interviews, work suspensions and/or termination. Whatever the work organization does in terms of discipline, the important thing is follow-through on established disciplinary procedures. The "action" is in the form of "constructive confrontation."

Referral is the action of getting the employee to the company EAP. This is done directly or through the organization's medical department. A brief description of the events and/or behavior leading to the referral should be documented and forwarded. The EAP counselor uses this as a tool in penetrating the employee's denial. A treatment plan is formulated by the counselor that might include inpatient treatment, outpatient treatment, or referral to an appropriate self-help program. The EAP counselor will continue to manage the case for at least one year.

Reintegration is particularly important when the employee is referred to an inpatient program. Returning to work can be an anxiety-provoking experience and is a crucial phase of the employee's recovery. This can be minimized if both supervisor and employee know what to expect.

THE UNION REPRESENTATIVE'S ROLE

Although the terms "job jeopardy," "constructive confrontation," and "documentation" are associated with management programs and the supervisory referral process, these steps in the intervention process are also used by shop stewards and business agents. The union representative is in a key position to identify the chemically dependent member even before the problem seriously affects job performance. As both a peer and a person who is in a position of authority, the representative's unique role lends itself to an effective constructive confrontation strategy—with concern. This applies whether or not the union has a formal program, management has a program, or a joint union-management program is operating. The union representative usually becomes aware of the problem through observation in the workplace, personal interaction with the individual, or feedback from other union members. An alert representative can frequently intervene in the earliest stages of dependency and affect recovery before the problem seriously affects the individual's family and job performance.[5]

Deteriorating job performance is management's concern, but it is also labor's concern. Work performance is a contractual issue. Union representatives interpret the contracts in their handling of labor-management problems and function as liaisons between labor and management. They are actively involved in the defining of the contract and facilitate employer-union relations. Early intervention, therefore, provides an opportunity for labor as well as for management. While only management has the right to terminate an employee for unacceptable work performance, the union can influence or prevent that decision.[6]

WORK-RELATED INCIDENTS VERSUS SYMPTOMS OF DEPENDENCY

Documentation of the troubled employee's deteriorating job performance is critical to an effective intervention. Work-related incidents should be noted and behavior directly related to the employee's responsibilities are the only kinds of information appropriate to the constructive confrontation. While there are many clinical symptoms that could manifest in the chemically dependent person, only those symptoms of deteriorating job performance should be discussed when confronting the employee. This is important for at least two reason: First, confronting those behaviors not directly related to job performance is irrelevant and might be considered discriminatory. The Federal Rehabilitation Act of 1973 protects the alcoholic and drug abuser from discrimination and using information other than job performance may be in violation of this act. Second, while the supervisor may be aware of other non-work-related symptoms, the supervisor is not a clinician and should not attempt to diagnose the problem. Even when the supervisor is aware of the nature of the problem, it is better not to discuss it. The intervention is more likely to be a success if the supervisor sticks with what a supervisor knows best: job performance.

THE DOs AND THE DON'Ts

This is generally the approach to an effective confrontation as applied by most work organizations. In addition, there are some DOs and DON'Ts that the supervisor must keep in mind.

DO:
  Let the employee know that work performance is the company's primary concern.
  Be aware that the problem will usually get worse without professional help.
  Emphasize confidentiality when making the referral.
  Explain that accepting a referral to the EAP will not necessarily exclude the employee from disciplinary procedures.
  Be specific as to what is expected from the employee in terms of job performance.
  Be objective, fair, consistent, and decisive.

DON'T:
  Diagnose—leave that job to the EAP.
  Discuss personal problems.
  Moralize—keep the confrontation to job performance.
  Counsel or be misled by emotional pleas.
  Cover up for a friend.

The supervisor's cooperation is essential to the success of the employee assistance program. Unless the supervisor knows how to conduct a constructive confrontation, prepare in advance so that it will be a success, and make a timely referral, the troubled employee will be deprived of the opportunity to get help and the opportunity to return to normal functioning. If a lack of such supervisory skills is organization-wide, then the EAP will fail. In order to prevent this failure, supervisors must learn the techniques and the process. Rather than firing or transferring troubled employees to other departments to "get rid" of the problem, the EAP deals with the problem in a direct manner, reducing chemical dependency throughout the organization. The following quote emphasizes the importance of the supervisor's role:

> The emergence of Occupational Alcoholism Programs (OAPs) not only provides a new mechanism for responding to employees with drinking problems, but also brings a new set of roles and responsibilities to the work environment. While the employee is the client of concern, the primary responsibility for the success of OAPs rests on the shoulders of supervisors.[7]

While this statement was made almost two decades ago, it still holds true today. Supervisors are key to the EAP's success. In training supervisors to use the EAP effectively, their supervisory skills are also fine-tuned. This is as true in the 1990s as it was in the 1940s.

PROGRAM'S SUCCESS REDUCES SUPERVISOR'S AMBIVALENCE

The role of the supervisor applies whether the program is an EAP or an OAP. The supervisor can be either a part of the problem or a part of the solution. If the problem is ignored, then there is no chance for solution. This point is stressed because it is easier to ignore the problem than to deal with it appropriately. The supervisor may be competent and run a "tight ship" in every way, yet when personal problems are the cause of an employee's deteriorating job performance, all systems break down. The supervisor may feel that the problem is none of his or her business and that getting involved would be meddling. But job performance *is* the supervisor's business and getting involved where performance is deteriorating is the supervisor's job.

Reluctance to deal with deteriorating job performance that might be related to personal problems is not uncommon. The supervisor may sympathize with the troubled employee, identify with the employee's problems, or be under the misconception that drinking is a solution to this employee's problems rather than the cause. Sometimes the supervisor's own drinking behavior, while not problematic, is an obstacle, such as, "How can I confront this employee when I probably drink more." This is where the supervisor's understanding of the procedures for identifying and referring the employee are important: that it is not the drinking or drug use being confronted but rather the employee's poor job performance.

During a recent discussion I had with supervisors who had been promoted out of the rank and file, several admitted that they had some difficulty in confronting and referring employees to the organization's EAP. Even though they knew the referral would be based strictly on deteriorating job performance, their addressing the problem was made more difficult by the fact that they knew what the real problem was. This was particularly true where alcohol was the troubled employee's drug of choice. A few of the supervisors drank themselves, very often with the employees they supervised, and felt they could not confront the employee without encroaching on the individual's personal life.

The supervisor is often not that far removed socially from the person supervised, and a confrontation may be perceived as the end of a friendship. This is not likely to happen. A constructive confrontation may actually be, in fact, the beginning of a relationship built on professional concern rather than on coverup. The following is an example of one such case:

A unit manager recently told me that one of her administrative assistants had been promoted to the position of assistant manager. I knew the woman who received the promotion because she had been referred by the manager to our EAP twenty-two months earlier. The EAP counselor assessed the case at that time and referred her to a rehabilitation program for twenty-eight days. She was a multi-substance abuser whose job performance showed a consistent pattern of deterioration. After completing the 28–day rehabilitation program, she enrolled in a continuing-care outpatient program that included group therapy, family counseling, and involvement in self-help groups. The employee responded very well to the EAP's treatment plan, obviously, demonstrating her ability to recover and return, once again, to full productivity.

That's a short story with a happy ending. There is another story, however, within that story. The unit manager who had conducted the constructive confrontation with this troubled employee expressed her ambivalence to me at that time. She perceived the employee to be "shy and troubled" and feared that "reprimanding" her poor job performance at this time would make matters worse. The employee, nevertheless, was not getting her job done. The manager overcame her ambivalence, however, with one training session. After learning the strategies and techniques involved, she conducted an effective constructive confrontation and executed a successful referral to the EAP.

While it did not take long for the manager to realize the success of her intervention, this success was reinforced by a verbal expression of gratitude from the employee. Fourteen months after the constructive confrontation and referral to the EAP took place, the employee went back to the unit manager and said:

> I was very angry at the time. I felt I had been betrayed and could no longer depend on you to cover up my problem. I was aware of the medical department's employee assistance program and knew that's where I'd be referred. I also knew, however, that I'd be able to manipulate the EAP and was planning my strategy even as you were confronting each incident of poor job performance. Boy, was I wrong—on both scores. The EAP had a "plan" for me that made me look like an amateur manipulator. As for your taking the action that you did, all I can say is thank you. That was the turning point in my life.

These remarks capture the essence of how most troubled employees feel after being referred to the EAP. The clinical and/or assessment skills of the EAP counselor in combination with the leverage that "job jeopardy" provides makes the employee an excellent candidate for rehabilitation. The troubled employee is also a troubled person whose problem extends far beyond the workplace, and is often relieved, in fact, that finally it must be dealt with. This is an opportunity—the employee realizes in retrospect—to lift a burden that would probably have been troubling the employee for years. Without the combined efforts of the supervisor and the EAP counselor, this opportunity may never have presented itself.

JOB JEOPARDY IS AN EAP TOOL

This approach to dealing with alcohol and drug related job performance problems is sometimes referred to as the "job jeopardy" model. To be totally effective, "job discipline" and "constructive confrontation" procedures should be an integral function of the program.[8] This approach imposes penalties that ultimately lead to termination if the chemical-dependent employee refuses, discontinues, or does not respond to the EAP's efforts. The employee must also maintain a satisfactory job-performance level.

Since one of the first signs of chemical dependency is a pattern of deteriorating job performance, the place of employment is a logical place to address the problem. Early recognition and intervention usually results in a more promising prognosis and successful rehabilitation. If a chemically dependent employee is permitted to deteriorate without any serious steps being taken to confront and resolve the problem, then so too will work performance deteriorate. It is necessary for the supervisor to be thoroughly trained in recognizing patterns of declining job performance, in maintaining documentation that supports these observations and in conducting a timely intervention and referral to the EAP.

ATTITUDES AND PREJUDICES INHIBIT THE PROCESS

Stereotyping inhibits case finding in the workplace while misconceptions about chemically dependent persons are barriers to EAP utilization. These misconceptions are reflected in the terms used to identify alcoholics and drug abusers. "There's nothing worse than a reformed drunk," for example, conjures the image of a self-righteous, proselytizing teetotaler, imposing his or her newly found sobriety in an uncompromising manner on anyone within earshot. This less-than-complimentary perception of the recovering alcoholic not only does nothing to remove the alcoholics undeserved reputation as a weak-willed individual who cannot hold liquor, but also identifies an obnoxious person to be avoided even when sober. Other expressions such as "He's on the wagon," or "She's off the sauce," suggest they'll soon fall off the wagon and be back on the sauce. Derisive labels such as "pillhead," "junkie," "speed freak," and "crackhead" do little to identify drug addiction as an illness.

While we are not likely to hear these expressions as often today, the underlying attitudes and misconceptions about the alcoholic and drug abuser are still held by many; and even though considerable progress has been made in educating the public to the fact that both alcoholism and drug abuse are treatable illnesses, these concepts have not been embraced by all. In a recent poll conducted at a shopping mall, several randomly selected pedestrians were asked how they felt about alcoholics and drug abusers. While their responses reflected a growing awareness about the nature of the problem, skepticism about the disease concept and the chance of recovery were also present. Some expressed the opinion that sobriety was a matter of self-control and others had little faith in the recovery of drug abusers. When asked what they thought about women who drank too much or used drugs, they were even less forgiving—sex, promiscuity, and shades of moral indecency were the attitudes that prevailed among many.

In a training session designed to help supervisors identify and refer troubled employees to the company EAP, I asked the participants to write down single words they associated with alcoholics and drug abusers. Although words such as illness, recovery and disease were mentioned, their responses also included drunk, dope, booze, weak, untrustworthy, dry, violence, jail and so on.

The point here is that the prevailing attitudes of society are also the prevailing attitudes of business and industry. This is not to say that society should suddenly "like" drug addicts and alcoholics, or that existing misconceptions should make way for new information presenting them in a different light. On the contrary, business and industry should continue to "dislike" chemically dependent persons and view them as personal and financial liabilities. But it should also recognize that chemical dependency, like diabetes, is a treatable disease and that rehabilitation may prove a good investment. This does not mean that employers should hire active alcoholics and drug abusers, but an effort should be made to reach those already employed whose job performance is deteriorating because of such problems.

PROBLEM DENIAL AFFECTS ALL CONCERNED

Reaching the chemically dependent person is sometimes easier said than done. Denial of the problem is a major obstacle to getting help for the drug or alcohol abuser. Unlike the diabetic who is likely to agree to treatment once the disease is diagnosed, the chemically dependent person clings to the notion that "control" is possible. Even those friends and relatives who are close to the individual frequently deny the problem. A typical refrain might be, "Mary's not an alcoholic, but she does drink too much sometimes." Using a variety of excuses and rationales, the chemically dependent person will attempt to convince all concerned that the matter is under control.[9] Retorts such as "I don't drink any more than my friends do," or "I can part company with cocaine any time I choose to," or "Valium helps me get through the day" are not uncommon. There may be an element of truth in these excuses. Many alcoholics do not drink much, some drug abusers *can* stop for days at a time, and prescription drug misusers are not always aware of the seriousness of their problem. The problem, nevertheless, is evident in how it affects the individual's social/family relationships, health, or job performance.

Not only does denial of the problem make it difficult for the "helper" to offer help, but the fact that the chemically dependent person becomes very skilled in convincing others that the problem really does not exist compounds it. This leaves the "helper," whether family member, friend or supervisor, feeling frustrated and helpless—emotions not conducive to continued efforts to offer assistance. All parties concerned tend to ignore the problem, hoping it will go away. They seldom have enough information early in the progression of the illness and, when it is finally out of control, the tendency is to cover up rather than confront. One reason for this is that once the problem is out in the open, someone has to find a solution. That responsibility usually falls upon whoever first abandons the notion that it might go away and admits, "We have a problem that must be confronted."

These dynamics apply both in the home and in the workplace. Many alcoholics have drunk themselves to death while friends, coworkers, family members, and supervisors hoped the problem might one day disappear. It is seldom a lack of concern that permits this to happen, but rather a lack of ability to turn concern into constructive action. In the workplace this ability comes in the form of a two-hour training program on identifying and referring the troubled employee to the EAP. It is here that the supervisor learns to store away whatever he or she knows about the employee's drug use, alcohol use, or personal problems, and applies the formula that has proven most effective in getting troubled employees back to full productivity once again: observation, documentation, confrontation, and referral. The supervisor's denial is diminished once the training is conducted, while the employee's denial is penetrated once the intervention takes place.

THE ROLE AND FUNCTION OF THE EAP COUNSELOR

The EAP counselor is the person responsible for seeing to it that the troubled employee receives the help necessary to correct the problem. This person may be a certified employee assistance professional, a certified social worker, a credentialed alcoholism/drug abuse counselor, a psychologist, a psychiatrist, a nurse trained in counseling, or a person holding credentials in any combination of these disciplines. The EAP may employ a full complement of professionals from various disciplines, such as psychiatry, psychology, social work, and counseling, or have only one person who assesses the problem and refers the employee to the appropriate outside resources(s) for assistance. The EAP counselor, whatever his or her professional credentials, is ultimately responsible for the troubled employee's treatment planning and/or knowing what treatment approach might be best applied.

Although some EAPs are prepared to provide a wide range of in-house services for the chemically dependent employee, including a medical examination, ambulatory detoxification, counseling and psychotherapy, most EAPs are not. Assessment, referral and follow-up counseling is more typical. The counselor is responsible for coordinating treatment efforts, monitoring job performance through contact with the supervisor, and providing ongoing motivational and supportive counseling. This person must have the qualifications needed to identify the problem and carry out those tasks critical to its solution. These tasks can be identified as follows:

1. To overcome the employee's denial of the problem.
2. To motivate a change in behavior.
3. To get the employee into appropriate treatment, when needed.
4. To facilitate re-entry into normal roles after treatment.
5. To provide social supports to facilitate efforts to change behavior.
6. To monitor progress of the employee's change efforts and establish two-way feedback on results.[10]

These are the clinical functions of the EAP counselor that are important to successful treatment outcomes. The counselor must know what techniques will best penetrate the employee's resistance and then turn that resistance into motivation. A knowledge of treatment resources and when to use them is essential. It is important, for example, that the counselor not overuse inpatient rehabilitation programs. A twenty-eight–day rehabilitation experience can be a very powerful treatment tool, but its therapeutic benefits are limited. Its value, to a great extent, is in the learning experience it provides. This value diminishes with overuse, however, and the experience could instead become an "escape" from the job and from life's challenges. Continuing care after discharge in an outpatient clinic is necessary.

Facilitating the employee's re-entry is a very important function that is frequently overlooked. It involves the supervisor, the employee, and the counselor. The employee must be counseled to facilitate the return to work after being away from the job for any length of time. If not handled skillfully, this could become a traumatic experience for the recovering person. The employee is vulnerable at this point, afraid of rejection, probing questions, and the fear of not being able to say no to a drug or drink if offered. The supervisor needs guidance in handling the situation professionally so as not to undermine the progress that has been made.

Providing social supports and monitoring the employee's progress is an ongoing task for the counselor. Long-term treatment skills are important here if the counselor is assuming the role of clinical case manager. If this function is left to an outside service provider, then the skill lies in knowing where motivational counseling ends and therapy begins. Under the best of circumstances, the counselor's role is ambiguous. A study on the subject of program functions indicated that the actual responsibilities of the counselor are so broad that "broker" is the best description. The study concludes:

> The core knowledge areas encompass alcohol/drug issues as well as emotional and relationship issues. Beyond these the EAP counselor may need some knowledge in the legal, financial, or medical fields. Perhaps the two most needed skills in EAP counselors are ability to relate to a wide variety of people and ability to do quick, reasonably non-threatening assessments. If an EAP program provides counseling in-house, then counselors need to be good counselors as well as good assessors.[11]

The EAP counselor is a professional and, like any professional, must know his or her limitations. This includes recognizing a problem that cannot be solved, and knowing where to look for help. The counselor should be capable of identifying behavior that does not fit the profile of a chemically dependent person, and knowing what resources will pick up where the EAP leaves off. When there is any question as to what the employee's problem may be, the employee must be referred to a resource capable of making that determination. In this sense, "broker" is an excellent description of an EAP counselor.

NOTES

1. "How Two Companies Curb Drug Abuse," *Occupational Hazards* (April 1983): 95.

2. Discussion with Harrison M. Trice, New York State School of Industrial and Labor Relations, Cornell University, Ithaca, NY, August 1983.

3. Mobil Oil Corporation, "Alcohol & Drug Abuse Program Manual," 1978, 1, (offset).

4. H.M. Trice and J.M. Beyer, "Social Control in Work-Settings: Using the Constructive Confrontation Strategy with Problem-Drinking Employees," *Journal of Drug Issues* ILR Reprint, Cornell University (Spring 1982): 21.

5. Madeleine L. Tramm, "Union-Based Programs," in *The Human Resources Management Handbook/Principles and Practice of Employee Assistance Programs*, ed. Samuel H. Klarreich and James L. Francek and C. Eugene Moore (New York: Praeger, 1985), 97.

6. Ibid.

7. Norma R. Kurta, Bradley Googins, and Carol N. Williams, "Supervisors' Views of an Occupational Alcoholism Program," *Alcohol Health and Research World* 4, No. 3 (Spring 1980): 44.

8. Harold V. Schmitz, *The Handbook of Employee Counseling Programs* (New York: New York Business Group on Health, 1982), 27.

9. Harry Milt, *The Revised Basic Handbook on Alcoholism* (Maplewood, NJ: Scientific Aids, 1977), 22.

10. Janice M. Beyer and Harrison M. Trice, "Design and Implementation of Job-Based Alcoholism Programs: Constructive Confrontation Strategies and How They Work," *NIAAA Research Monograph No. 8/Occupational Alcoholism: A review of Research Issues* (Rockville, MD: 1981): 181, 182.

11. Judy M. Winkelpleck, "Directions EAPs Move," *EAP Digest* (July/August 1984): 19.

6

Managed Health Care Versus Managed Health Costs

BENEFITS EXPENDITURES ON THE RISE

Employer costs for mental health and substance abuse treatment are increasing more rapidly than for any other segment of health care. As discussed in previous chapters, employers face both direct and indirect costs due to mental health and substance abuse problems. Direct costs are not difficult to quantify. The Foster Higgins' 1988 Health Care Benefits Survey reported that the mental health care portion of a company's overall medical expenditure averaged 9.6 percent. Other studies report figures as high as 25 percent.[1] Indirect costs are those that affect company efficiency and may double or even triple the total costs associated with mental health and substance abuse.[2]

The Foster Higgins' Survey reported that in companies of more than five thousand employees, the cost of providing psychiatric and substance abuse benefits increased 47 percent in 1989 to $297 per employee. In companies of any size, the cost increased 18 percent, to $244 per employee. In 1988, the previous year, the cost rose 27 percent.[3] At this rate of increase, we might expect the cost to be more than $350 per employee in 1992. To put this in perspective, a company with five thousand employees will be paying $1.75 million for psychiatric and substance abuse benefits alone!

Over the past several years, the demand for treatment services has been increasing dramatically. A number of factors are responsible for this phenomenon. They include increasingly stressful lifestyles, greater availability of mental health benefits and decreased stigma attached to mental health service use. It is estimated that 18.7 percent of Americans over age 18 have some type of psychiatric disorder and 6.4 percent suffer from substance abuse problems.[4]

ENTER MANAGED CARE

In response to the increasing demand for mental health and substance abuse services, business and industry began to monitor expenditures. In a study conducted by CNA Insurance, mental health and substance abuse services accounted for a disproportionate utilization rate. Inpatient utilization for such services increased 25 percent between 1985 and 1987 while all other inpatient utilization rates actually decreased. The average cost for mental health and substance abuse expenditures per patient was actually twice that of surgical![5] With these and other such alarming studies came a flurry of activities aimed at reducing the high cost of providing benefits. These "activities" have come to be known as "managed care."

Managed care (MC) is an insurance product that attempts to balance cost of services with quality of care. It is a systematic effort to contain the rising cost of medical, psychiatric, and chemical dependency treatment through employer-based efforts.[6] MC may represent one or a combination of benefit incentives and/or disincentives designed to minimize or eliminate unnecessary health care provider services. Its objective—to reduce health care benefit expenditures—is achieved through such cost-containment measures as reviewing cases prior to hospital admission (precertification), requiring second surgical opinions, conducting concurrent case reviews, and using financial incentives encouraging outpatient rather than inpatient services, when possible. A managed care program may also impose an annual dollar limit on treatment services, use physicians as gatekeepers, establish preferred provider organizations (PPO), or contract with health maintenance organizations (HMO). An employee assistance program (EAP) is often a component of a comprehensive managed care plan.

MANAGED CARE BY ANY OTHER NAME

Managed care appears in the literature under several different names. They include:

Managed health care
Managed care programming
Managed mental health care

Managed behavioral health care
Utilization management

The name to be used interchangeably throughout this chapter will be "managed care," or its abbreviation "MC." An MC program, company, component, and so on, will be identified simply as "MC." Managed care or MC will refer specifically to the management of mental health, alcoholism, and other drug abuse treatment and costs. It will not include medical care. This exclusion serves to eliminate awkward qualifiers such as "the mental health, alcoholism, and drug abuse treatment monitoring function of a managed care program." Since MC "carves out" mental health and chemical dependency benefits from total health care benefits, this application is accurate.

Well-planned MC attempts to contain the cost of mental health services through cost-effective quality care. It searches for and develops delivery systems that save money without sacrificing quality. Many employers have demonstrated success in their MC efforts while others are still studying the results of their efforts. The jury is, in fact, still out. Respondents in a recent survey of employee benefits managers showed that only 7 percent reported an absolute decrease in expenditures through MC. The same survey shows, however, that 75 percent of the respondents did report a lower rate of benefits cost increase. Still again, 14 percent noted no change![7] Another study conducted by consultant A. Foster Higgins & Co., Inc., reported that 55 percent of the benefits managers surveyed were unable to measure the effect their PPO arrangements have had on their overall health care costs.[8]

WHO DOES MANAGED CARE AND HOW

Managed care is done by:

1. An insurance carrier.
2. A managed care service company.
3. An employee-assistance program contractor with a managed care component.
4. A self-insured organization or union trust fund with a managed care component.

According to the General Counsel for the National Association of Addiction Treatment Providers (NAATP), managed care programs have four key components:

1. *Preferred provider networks* (negotiated fees, quality care, specific service agreements)
2. *Utilization management* (benefits plan design, pre-authorization for treatment, case management including concurrent and retrospective patient review)
3. *Data collection and analyses*
4. *Quality-control systems*[9]

A managed care program must have these four components in place if care and costs are to be successfully controlled. MC is not feasible without agreements with treatment service facilities providing quality care at competitive costs. With this component in place, utilization management follows. Case management becomes easier when the treatment service provider and the referring organization understand each other's requirements, and when the insured person understands the conditions of the benefit plan. Unfortunately, most people know little about health insurance coverage, often assuming that whatever treatment their doctor renders or recommends will be covered.

Data collection and analyses is critical to the success of any managed care program. This should not only include cost data but also effectiveness data.

Quality control is the logical completion of the managed care component quadrant. Studies are important to the success of an MC in that it provides information on both the level of care used and the performance of the provider of treatment services. While treatment programs should be expected to conduct follow-up studies, the best outcome studies are conducted by the referring organizations and/or the MC component. An employee assistance program responsible for assessment, referral, and case management is in a position where it can establish criteria and evaluate a treatment program's effectiveness. If, for example, 40 percent of the employees completing treatment at Surecure Center are relapsing six months after discharge while the relapse rate for Lastchance Center discharges is 11 percent, all other factors considered, Lastchance is the more cost-effective program. This is one way in which an EAP can be a critical component of MC.

The Employee Assistance Professionals Association, Inc., released in 1990 a monograph that addresses the issue of MC and employee assistance programs. Titled *Maximizing Behavioral Health Benefit Value through EAP Integration*, this work provides information for the consumer of managed care services.

A GAME WITH SEVERAL PLAYERS

Health care began as a two-party relationship, a patient and a doctor. The doctor controlled the type of and access to treatment. The treatment provider or hospital became an extension of the doctor's services. As the cost of care rose and became a burden for the unfortunate individual, a third party, the insurance carrier became a player. Group plans became an economical way to offer coverage, and employers became the largest purchasers of insurance plans. As utilization escalated and premiums increased, third party insurance carries responded by introducing a "fourth party": managed care.

Health care is hardly a subject to be treated with levity. Illness, including chemical dependency, is no laughing matter and the cost of treatment today is not a joke. Yet, with the introduction of managed care, health care has taken on the characteristics of a challenging board game. The players are patients, doctors, providers, purchasers, insurers and MC reviewers.

> The *patients* are employees seeking treatment under the coverage of a managed care plan.
>
> The *doctors* provide care and facilitate treatment plans.
>
> The *providers* are the doctors, programs, or hospitals providing treatment.
>
> The *purchasers* are the employers or labor unions that buy group health plans.
>
> The *insurers* are insurance companies, health maintenance organizations, in-house insurance plans, preferred provider organizations, etc.
>
> The *MC reviewers* are the persons (managed care service companies, etc.) assigned the task to "manage" the chemical dependency treatment.

Most rules in the treatment coverage game are written by the insurance carrier. Many insurance carriers have either implemented their own MC function or turned the rule book over to an MC company (program, component, etc). The irony is that the MC is also a participant in the game. As the case reviewer, it gives MC an unfair advantage in the game. The MC determines whether or not the client (patient, employee, etc.) will be covered for chemical dependency treatment and whether or not the treatment program will be paid for its services. The MC also controls the actual budget to be spent on mental health and chemical dependency treatment.

Because many MCs enter into contracts with purchasers on a "risk assumption" basis, the more money they save the purchaser the more money they earn for themselves. In its simplest form, an MC company will contract with an organization to reduce its chemical dependency and mental health benefit expenditures. This is accomplished by implementing cost-containment measures discussed earlier in the chapter. If the contractor achieves the agreed-upon financial objective, it realizes a profit. If it does not, it assumes the risk and takes a loss.

MC reviewers make decisions based on accepted standards of care. Medical care has standards that are accepted and recognized throughout the country. Mental health and especially chemical dependency problems pose a challenge. Diagnoses of such problems are elusive and treatment choices may vary considerably. It should be noted that medical and even psychiatric standards evolved from traditional medical research and technology. Alcohol and drug recovery services, however, evolved from grassroots efforts of recovering people attempting to help each other.[10] As alcoholism became "medicalized," inpatient rehabilitation recovery services and the twelve-step treatment approach became more "professional."[11]

The nontraditional nature of the twelve-step treatment approach has posed both a challenge to traditional medicine and a dilemma for third-party insurers. The dilemma, to pay or not to pay, engages all the players in the game. If the MC reviewer determines that a prescribed treatment plan is not necessary, the prescribing physician or treatment provider may be ethically responsible to carry out that treatment plan. If it is carried out, is the treating physician or treatment provider legally entitled to payment from the patient? If the treatment plan is not carried out, who is liable in the event of personal damages?

Theoretically, both the MC and the treating physician should operate under the same standards of medical necessity, which by definition should be determined by the community standard of care. But as discussed above, standards in the treatment of chemical dependency disorders are nebulous. At the heart of the liability debate is the fundamental question of who should bear the risk of MC decisions; whether and how that risk can be allocated without resorting to legal confrontation. A secondary, but perhaps more immediate, question is how to provide for expedient reviews of MC decisions so that bad decisions can be reversed before they impact on patient care.[12] While this has not yet evolved as a pressing issue in the area of chemical-dependency treatment, if the current trends continue, it will.

MENTAL HEALTH INPATIENT TREATMENT CRITERIA

Standard mental health (excluding substance abuse) treatment protocol for inpatient hospitalization is widely accepted. The criteria are:

Possible homicide or suicide
Imminent threat of physical harm
Life-threatening medical conditions

If these conditions are not present, alternative treatment options are considered. These include less expensive residential care, including halfway houses or partial hospitalization programs. Outpatient treatment is usually the least costly alternative.

SUBSTANCE ABUSE INPATIENT TREATMENT CRITERIA

Substance abuse treatment protocol is less specific and more interpretive. Three patient categories determine treatment settings:

Addictive behavior brought on by sudden trauma in a person who functioned on a high level before the trauma. Prognosis is good and the person should respond well to intensive outpatient treatment.

Addictive behavior brought on by sudden trauma or chronic substance abuse is someone with average pre-illness functioning. Prognosis is guarded but, with early intervention (an argument for EAPs) and proper motivation, a person should respond to intensive outpatient or partial hospitalization (day program) with followup aftercare.

Chronic substance abuse in a person demonstrating poor pre-illness functioning. Recovery for this group is dubious but, with proper motivation and support systems, a person can achieve cure. The three step protocol includes: inpatient detoxification (no more than seven days); residential treatment; and most important, structured followup and care to prevent repeat hospitalizations.[13]

SUBSTANCE ABUSE VERSUS MENTAL HEALTH CRITERIA

Inpatient admission criteria for mental health treatment is relatively straightforward. "Homicide," "suicide," and "life threatening" are the key words. For substance abuse, however, there are several qualifiers that will support a decision for outpatient over inpatient care. "The person should respond," "proper motivation," "with early intervention," and "with support systems" are a few. With the exception of the term "pre-illness functioning," there does not appear to be definitive criteria for inpatient hospitalization. If the person had "high" or "average" pre-illness functioning, outpatient treatment would be the modality of choice. If the person demonstrates "poor" pre-illness functioning, hospitalization would be indicated.

The concept of "pre-illness functioning" is somewhat elusive. It assumes that alcoholism and drug abuse is a symptom of a pre-existing condition where functioning is also a symptom of that condition. It seems to ignore the fact that both alcoholism and drug addiction are disease entities and that the pre-morbid condition, unless a dual diagnosis of mental illness and chemical dependency is present, may actually be a stage in the development of the disease.

Additionally, qualifiers such as "pre-illness functioning," "proper motivation," and so on are too vague and interpretive. Such "standards" allow both the MC reviewer and the treatment service provider too many opportunities to defend their position. If the provider is presenting a case for inpatient treatment, the prognosis is "dubious" and the patient will need "proper motivation" and "support systems" to ensure a successful outcome. The reviewer, on the other hand, might deny inpatient care arguing that the client's motivation and support systems indicate outpatient care as the treatment of choice.

The problems in meeting the criteria for inpatient treatment notwithstanding, both inpatient treatment service providers and EAP counselors are often not properly prepared in presenting a treatment plan, including the rationale for their choice of treatment, to the MC reviewer. The case is often presented in such a way that the diagnosed individual does not satisfy the criteria for inpatient hospitalization even when, in fact, he or she does. Satisfying these criteria, however, is not simply a matter of placing the square peg in the square hole. National standards to which the employee assistance program, the treatment program, and the managed care program can refer have not existed A treatment plan based on any published criteria governing inpatient admissions is better than no plan at all. If "pre-illness functioning," "motivation," and "support" are the qualifiers for determining treatment choices, then the case must be presented in terms of these variables.

TREATMENT CRITERIA ENDORSED BY EAP ASSOCIATION

The "Criteria for Levels of Care for Psychoactive Substance Use Disorders," prepared by the St. Louis Chapter of Employee Assistance

Professionals Association (EAPA, formerly ALMACA) Insurance Committee, and drawn, in part, from National Association of Addiction Treatment Programs (NAATP) information, establishes criteria by which patients are referred to the appropriate level of care to ensure effective utilization from both clinical and cost perspectives. General criteria for levels of treatment as determined through a medical examination are:

1. The patient will be admitted to the least restrictive treatment environment possible.
2. Patient will be moved to the least restrictive treatment environment as soon as therapeutically feasible.[14]

The [edited] EAPA criteria for admission to inpatient hospital/residential setting with comprehensive medical care available include:

A. Provisional diagnosis. At least three of the following are needed:
   1. Psychoactive substance taken over longer period of time than the person intended
   2. Unsuccessful in cutting down usage
   3. Much time and activity spent in getting, taking or recovering from drug's effects
   4. Frequent intoxication or withdrawal interferes with functioning
   5. Important functions given up because of usage
   6. Continued usage despite consequences
   7. Marked tolerance
   8. Characteristic withdrawal symptoms (DSM-III-R)
   9. Drug taken to avoid withdrawal symptoms
B. Factors for medical detoxification. Documented history of both of the following needed:
   1. High probability of medical complication during intoxication, i.e., acutely intoxicated
   2. Increased tolerance or withdrawal symptoms
C. Factors for inpatient hospital/residential treatment. One of the following necessary:
   1. Medical complications
   2. Major psychiatric illness
   3. Failure of outpatient treatment
   4. Severe psychological, social, or occupational dysfunction

If the employee assistance professional or the treatment program professional does a thorough assessment and the case clearly indicates inpatient treatment as the "least restrictive" treatment alternative at the time of intake or recertification, the treatment plan is likely to be accepted by the MC reviewer. This seemingly logical conclusion makes three assumptions, however. First, that the MC reviewer is professionally qualified to review drug and alcohol abuse treatment cases; second, that the MC reviewer is utilizing treatment standards to approve or deny treatment; third, that the MC's primary objective is "care" and not "cost" management.

This may not always be the case. While it would be naive to believe that MC's exclusive objective is to provide the client with the best care available, a balance of cost effectiveness and quality care is achievable. This is possible only when both the reviewer and the provider are thoroughly familiar with both inpatient and out-patient admission standards. The following case study should be considered:

A health insurance carrier for several municipal agencies contracted with a managed care service company to monitor treatment for chemically dependent employees. Several of the municipal EAPs attempted to find out precisely what the MC's criteria were for accepting or rejecting employee claims. This author also asked the same question of the MC. The MC refused to answer. Their explanation was that it was not company policy to release such information.

It should be noted that managed care is a competitive business and, like any business, its competitors compete on all levels. Criteria used by MC reviewers in determining levels of care are developed through research. It is a function of the product they are selling to their clients (work organizations or insurance companies) and, understandably, has a business value. It stands to reason, then, that an MC would be reluctant to divulge these criteria. The first objective of a business is to stay in business, to stay competitive. Like any business, an MC must stay competitive. It must demonstrate its ability to be effective; to reduce costs for the clients it serves; and to do it better than the competition. Nevertheless, where health and healing are at stake, such criteria should not be kept secret.

GETTING THE CHEMICALLY DEPENDENT EMPLOYEE INTO TREATMENT

While there are many procedural applications of managed care, the following is typical:

1. An employee is referred to the employee assistance program because of poor job performance.
2. The EAP counselor determines that the employee has a chemical dependency problem and calls an inpatient rehabilitation treatment program to refer the employee to.
3. The treatment program checks the employee's insurance policy and learns that an MC is responsible for monitoring the chemical dependency/mental health benefits. (The EAP is not always aware of the insurance coverage of an employee. There are sometimes many different plans within one organization.)
4. The treatment program then calls the MC and is told that hospital pre-certification is required for all chemical dependency treatment cases; and that an independent physician must assess the case. The program is also told that a weekly re-certification is necessary (concurrent case review) in order to qualify for reimbursement.
5. The rehabilitation program contacts the EAP and advises the counselor of the conditions that must be met.
6. The counselor "finds" a physician and refers the employee for an evaluation.
7. The physician confirms the counselor's assessment and approves the admission.
8. The employee enters the treatment program. A weekly recertification (satisfying continuing inpatient care criteria) is submitted to the MC by the attending physician. Continuing inpatient treatment is determined by the reviewer.

Early in the chapter we offered some definitions for managed care. We described it as an insurance product that attempts to balance cost of services with quality of care. We also called it a systematic effort to contain the rising cost of medical, psychiatric, and chemical dependency treatment through employer-based efforts. At this point we can add still another, if somewhat lengthy, definition by the Committee on Utilization Management by Third Parties. Their definition is as follows:

> Managed Care is a set of techniques used by or on behalf of purchasers of health benefits to manage health care costs by influencing patient care decision-making through case-by-case assessments of the appropriateness of care prior to its provision.[15]

Managed care is a business approach to managing a human service. The language used to communicate about managed care is evidence of that. Words like "cost benefit," "cost effectiveness," "contract," "subscriber," "indemnify," "audit," "proactive," have entered the treatment literature and the vocabulary of the treatment professional. Business and industry is on the cost-containment bandwagon, with a focus on chemical dependency. Paradoxically, business and industry is also on the drug-free workplace bandwagon. On September 5, 1989, *The Wall Street Journal* ran an article titled "Firms Cut Drug-Treatment Benefits."[16] On that very same day, President Bush announced his initiatives on the war against drugs, citing the Drug-Free Workplace Act as the first step in working toward a drug-free society!

Employers, insurance carriers, treatment programs, employee assistance programs, and managed care service companies are scrambling to do the right thing, whatever that is. The spirit of competition came alive in the health care field in the 1970s as hospitals and treatment professionals learned the value of strategic marketing. The emergence of chemical dependency treatment programs in the 1980s and the escalating cost of delivering such services created an inevitable search for referral sources. Emerging managed care cost containment efforts are reducing utilization rates, reducing the length of stays and creating an ever-increasing competitive environment. The treatment industry and some independent analysts worry that shorter stays will result in fewer successful outcomes. The readmission rate within six months of initial treatment is 15.5 percent for inpatient rehabilitation lasting 15 to 24 days, almost twice the readmission rate for longer stays, according to a study by Medstat Systems, Inc.[17]

Both voluntary and proprietary treatment programs are positioning themselves and expanding their marketing efforts. Outpatient treatment programs are competing against inpatient treatment program and inpatient treatment programs are competing against each other. Everybody is competing with psychiatric hospitals.

Ironically, managing the cost and treatment of chemically dependent employees is not a new idea. A well designed employee assistance program *is* managed care. As discussed in previous chapters, the EAP is a cost-effective early intervention system designed to help troubled employees with problems that interfere with their ability to function on the job. The EAP is an effective gatekeeper, identifying troubled employees early on and referring them to the appropriate level of care.

The key term in measuring the EAP's ability to serve as a function of managed care is "well designed." Just as a benefit plan must be well designed to promote efficient utilization, an EAP must be well designed to function effectively. While most EAPs do the job they are designed to do, some may not. One critic cited EAPs as "enemies of health care and cost containment." In a *Business Insurance* article, the writer describes the EAP as an excellent idea that has gotten out of control. Citing such issues as poor management and inexperienced counselors, the argument presented was that the EAP often functions on a low corporate level and does not understand the communications, politics, or objectives of business. Consequently, it refers troubled employees to treatment cavalierly, without regard to treatment costs. The article also said that EAPs often receive "bounties" from treatment programs for referrals. Some treatment programs even hire EAP counselors as "consultants" as a ploy to generate referrals. Finally, the writer proposed scrapping the EAP system and going back to the drawing board with a design that would include the managed care concept.[18]

The critic makes some important points. All EAPs are not cost effective, some lack professional integrity, and others engage in questionable "preferred provider" practices. While some EAPs may engage in practices that border on the unethical, such practices are probably in the minority. Nevertheless, the field has a responsibility to "police" itself to insure that the highest standards possible are maintained. Both the Employee Assistance Society of North America (EASNA) and the Employee Assistance Professionals Association (EAPA) developed program standards in 1990.

As for EAPs that are not managed effectively, such programs give both managed care and the EAP profession a bad name. The EAP objective is both functional and organizational. It helps the troubled employee while reducing the costly problem of chemical dependency. An EAP that functions marginally, however, should be challenged. Like any other department within any organization, it should be capable of demonstrating effectiveness in qualitative and quantitative terms. An EAP that can not show its value in dollars is not a well-designed program. Just as an MC would be expected to justify its contract through cost-benefit analysis, the value of the EAP should also be measurable. A recent study conducted by Alexander & Alexander Health Strategies Group (A&A), a Connecticut-based consulting firm, underscores the cost-effective potential of employee assistance programs. In this independently conducted study, the McDonnell Douglas Corporation's EAP showed typical savings-to-investment ratios of anywhere from 1.5:1 to 15:1. The total EAP cost offset (EAP annual cost savings minus annual program operating expense) was $2.5 million in 1987 and $3.9 million in 1988. This represents nearly a 3:1 return on investment (ROI) in 1987 and over a 4:1 ROI in 1988.

This cost study is particularly important for several reasons. First, because it was built on accepted statistical and scientific methodologies and conducted by an independent third party. Second, its data base was significantly larger than any similar EAP study to date. Third, it was a longitudinal study with outcomes examined over an extended period for each case. Fourth, A&A had access to all EAP health claims and personnel data in MDC. Finally, and perhaps most important, A&A did not try to measure the financial impact of factors which cannot be objectively and concretely measured. "Soft-dollar" items such as productivity, job performance level, replacement labor costs, and other subjective data were ignored. The only two items that were measured were actual health claims costs for the employee and family and absenteeism.[19]

Another important observation here is that the EAP study demonstrates cost benefit, not benefit savings. The study measures results by way of ROI whereas managed care is measuring expenditure reduction. This is not to say that a carefully planned and executed managed care program is not cost effective in the short run, but it will take a longitudinal managed care cost benefit study to prove its true managed care value. There are no such studies available.

A final comment on the EAP as a managed care component is that most MCs do not visit the chemical dependency treatment programs that they work with or refer to. They usually base their decision to include a facility in their panel of preferred treatment providers by reviewing information provided by the program. While confirmation of a facility's state license and national accreditation can be obtained in this manner, quality of care above and beyond such standards cannot. Employee assistance programs know this and are more likely to visit prospective treatment resources to determine whether or not the fit is right. The decision to use or not to use a treatment provider is based not just on the facility's ability to meet regulatory requirements, but on actual performance and results.

Cost containment and quality care, unfortunately, do not always make good bedfellows.[20] This does not mean that the idea should be tossed. The cost of care will always be a factor in making treatment decisions. It is important, however, that the most appropriate level of care not be compromised in the interest of cost containment. If it is, the employee will become another patient caught in the "revolving door," relapsing and reentering treatment time and again. Instead, the best possible treatment alternative at the lowest possible cost must be sought. In this way cost effective delivery systems that save money without sacrificing quality will emerge to give real meaning to the term "managed care."

NOTES

1. Glenn Kramon, "Employers Test New Ways to Shift Risk on Health Costs," *The New York Times,* June 22, 1988.

2. Robin B. Weiner and Debra Siegel, "Managed Mental Health Care Issues and Strategies," *Benefits Quarterly*, 5, No. 3 (Third Quarter 1989): 21–31.

3. Tim W. Ferguson, "Any Wonder Medical Premiums Are Anything But Shrinking?," *The Wall Street Journal*, May 22, 1990, A21.

4. *Mental Health, United States*, 1985, National Institute of Mental Health.

5. Weiner and Siegel, "Managed," *Benefits Quarterly:* 21–31.

6. Kathleen A. Sullivan, "Insurance Trends & Managed Care," presentation for the United Labor Agency, Newark, NJ, November 1990.

7. Census Results; "Topic: Issues in Managed Health Care," *Benefits Quarterly*, 5, No. 3 (Third Quarter 1989): 109–112.

8. Jerry Geisel, "Employers, PPOs Seek New Efficiences," *Business Insurance 1989–1990 Directory of HMOs and PPOs*, (December 1989): 6.

9. John L. Roberts, MEd, CEAP, and Micki Perez, ACSW, " 'Managing' Managed Care," *The Counselor*, (September/October 1989): 15–17.

10. Interview with Kathleen Sullivan, Health Benefits Research and Services Corporation, New York City, June 1, 1990.

11. "Twelve-Step" describes a model and recovery approach first introduced through Alcoholics Anonymous a self-help recovery program co-founded in 1935 by William Griffith Wilson (Bill W.) and Dr. Robert Holbrook Smith (Dr. Bob). These twelve steps of recovery have become the foundation of all "anonymous" groups that follow AA's principles.

12. Bradford H. Gray and Marilyn J. Field, *Controlling Costs and Changing Patient Care? The Role of Utilization Management* (Washington, DC: National Academy Press, 1989), 194–196.

13. Census, *Benefits Quarterly*, 1989.

14. Employee Assistance Professionals Association (EAPA, formerly ALMACA), St. Louis Chapter, "Criteria for Levels of Care for Psychoactive Substance Use Disorders." Based on criteria developed by the National Association of Addiction Treatment Programs (April 1988) (Photocopied).

15. Gray and Field, *Controlling Costs*, 2.

16. "Firms Cut Drug-Treatment Benefits," *The Wall Street Journal*, September 5, 1989; B1.

17. Kenneth H. Bacon, "Private Drug Abuse Treatment Centers Try to Adjust to Life in the Slow Lane," *The Wall Street Journal*, July 23, 1990; B1.

18. Dr. Walter E. Afield, "Running Amok: Employers Losing Control of EAP Costs, Management," *Business Insurance*, May 29, 1989.

19. "McDonnell Douglas Corporation's EAP Produces HARD DATA," *The ALMACAN*, 19, No. 8 (August 1989): 18–26.

20. William N. Penzer, PhD, "The Realities of Managed Mental Health Care," *EAP Digest*, January/February 1990; 35.

7

EAP Cost Benefits and Considerations

SUCCESS RATES ARE HIGH

It is estimated that 25 percent of the chemically dependent employee's earnings are lost to decreased productivity and poor job performance. It is also estimated that this employee will be absent three times more often than fellow employees, and that sickness and accident benefits will be paid at a rate three times greater than that of the national average. A current longitudinal report conducted by an independent consulting group confirms this finding showing that overall medical claims costs and absenteeism rates are at least twice that of the general employee population.[1]

The success of EAPs is demonstrated by the high recovery rates among employees who accept a referral for help rather than face disciplinary action for deteriorating job performance. This rate is estimated to be 50 percent, which means that at least half of all employees receiving EAP services will be returned to "full" productivity within one year.

A recent study shows that 62 percent of the working population consumes alcoholic beverages and 11 percent of that group drinks at least five days per week.[2] Another source reports that 36.6 percent of the population has used illicit mood-altering substances in the past and that 7.3 percent are current users.[3] These data support existing estimates that 5 to 15 percent of the working population are likely to have related problems serious enough to affect job performance and/or productivity.

If we assume a company with five thousand employees earning an average of $30,000 annually and apply some simple mathematics, we can see why most EAPs make good economic sense. Of the five thousand men and women in the company's employ, an estimated 70 percent, or 3,500 drink, and/or use drugs recreationally. Of this 3,500, at least 5 percent, or 175 employees, will exhibit problems related to this use and/or abuse. If we apply annual average earnings of $30,000 to these 175 employees, we have a figure of $5.25 million paid to this group.

Taking these total wages of $5.25 million paid annually to this group, and applying the estimated cost factor of 25 percent (absenteeism, medical expenses, disability claims, measurable productivity losses, lateness, and other quantifiable items), we have an estimated cost of $1,312,500 to the employer. Finally, if we assume an EAP recovery rate of 50 percent, then 50 percent of this $1,312,500 loss, or $656,250, could be saved in one year.

Formula For Savings
5,000 x .70 = 3,500 Drink and/or use drugs
3,500 x .05 = 175 Related problems
$30,000 x 175 = $5,250,000 Total salaries
$5,250,000 x .25 = $1,312,500 Cost to employer
$1,312,500 x .50 = $656,250 Saved thru EAP

This hypothetical exercise makes lots of assumptions, of course. It assumes that replacing the troubled employee would be more costly than rehabilitation. It assumes that the 50 percent success rate will restore these employees to 100 percent productivity. It assumes that there are no rehabilitation costs involved in the employee's recovery. The biggest assumption is that this entire population of troubled employees will be referred to the corporate employee assistance program. These projections, nevertheless, serve to provide a ballpark estimate of the cost of *not* having an employee assistance program. The savings realized when an EAP is in place depend upon a great many variables. Because it is difficult to isolate all the variables essential to a "true" cost-benefit analysis, there are not many such evaluations on employee assistance programs.[4] Nevertheless, those studies that have been published show a general agreement that EAPs reduce the cost of alcohol and drug related problems in the workplace.

COST BENEFIT VERSUS COST EFFECTIVENESS

Capital investments are usually made for one of two reasons: to generate profit or to reduce costs. Investing in an EAP serves the latter objective. As discussed earlier, the earliest occupational alcoholism programs were products of the "new campaign for scientific efficiency in industry." The Temperance Movement, Taylorism, and Workman's Compensation combined to drive alcohol from the workplace.[5] Two of these three influences, it can be noted, are directly related to costs and industry. Taylorism provided the first approach to scientific management and productivity measurement that associated costs and profit with time and motion. And before the passage of workers' compensation laws, an injured employee ordinarily had to file suit against an employer and prove that the injury was due to the employer's negligence. When these laws went into effect, however, the employee became eligible for compensation regardless of fault or blame. Drinking in the workplace, a problem that certainly affected productivity and costs, and was also responsible for many occupational accidents, became a serious concern to all corporate managers.

Cost containment remains an important measure of success for employee assistance programs. Whatever the humanistic value of an organization's EAP may be, a quantitative measure of the program's effectiveness is necessary to satisfy the rationale for such a program. Sometimes this is expressed in dollars saved (cost-benefit) and sometimes it takes the form of the success rates for employees helped (cost-effectiveness). The program can show, for example, that for every dollar invested, two dollars are saved, or that for every $25,000 invested, one-hundred troubled employees are reached. Whichever measure or combination of measures is used, the objective is to place a quantifiable value on the EAP function. While the ultimate measure of success is cost-benefit analysis, there are other ways to evaluate a program's effectiveness. The four most widely used are: (1) a change in drinking behavior; (2) work performance as revealed by disciplinary actions, accidents, sickness and injury days taken, turnover rate, and job efficiency; (3) cost efficiency, as revealed by direct savings for employers resulting from decreases in absenteeism and indirect saving such as increased accuracy of work; and (4) penetration rate, or the extent to which the program reaches its target population.[6]

While all four methods can be expressed in quantitative terms, (2) and (3) contain those categories of variables necessary to begin a *cost-benefit* analysis, that is, total savings/total investment costs. *Cost-effectiveness* is a relative measure of success therefore (1) and (4) could be used in this method of evaluation, that is, total employees helped/total investment costs. Cost-benefit could be viewed as an economic measure while cost-effectiveness might be considered both an economic and a humanistic measure of success.

The field of employee assistance programming abounds with literature attesting to the cost benefit of programs addressing the problem of chemical dependency in the workplace. Most of this literature is promotional, estimating savings based on projected macro-cost percentages. There are also several statistically significant studies, however, that show the cost benefit of having EAPs in place. The New York Transit Authority computed a savings of $1 million per year paid in sick leave benefits alone while General Motors boasts a 72 percent reduction in the dollar amount paid for accident and sickness disability benefits.[7]

The U.S.Postal Service showed an annual savings of over $2 million through their broad-brush EAP; New York Telephone claims $1.5 million and DuPont saw a return of a half-million dollars over and above its program costs. AT&T claims $448,000 in actual and anticipated savings annually.[8] One of the most important studies to date is an evaluation of the McDonnell Douglas Corporation's EAP. MDC commissioned the consulting firm of Alexander & Alexander Health Strategies Group to design and perform the study. What sets this study apart from the rest is that it is longitudinal, quantifiable, and current. Also critical to the credibility of this study is that it was built on accepted statistical and scientific methodologies and performed by an independent third party. It measures just two variables: actual health claims costs and absenteeism over a five-year period. Soft-dollar items such as productivity, job-performance level, replacement labor costs, and other subjective data were ignored.

The MDC study confirmed what earlier studies showed: that a well-managed EAP system results in significant cost reductions. The actual return-on-investment (ROI) for MDC was 4:1, four dollars saved for each dollar invested.[9] The study measured chemical dependency and psychiatric treatment separately for all employees and family members using EAP services versus those not using EAP services. A control group was also studied. These "control" employees were not treated at any time for either illness. Based on the results of this five-year study, the estimated offset value of the EAP over the *next* four year period will be $6 million. This will include $2.1 million in employee medical claims and $3 million in dependent medical claims. Absenteeism over the coming four years will be reduced by 7,761 days, producing an additional $900,000 in savings.

The actual study showed that the total five-year costs for EAP clients treated for chemical dependencies were, on the average, $7,150 lower than for those employees treated but did *not* use the EAP. Psychiatric case costs were $3,975 lower. Dependent medical claims costs offset for chemical dependency and psychiatric treatment over a four-year period were $14,728 and $8,762 lower, respectively.[10]

Projections of cost savings, as noted earlier, are used to determine the potential cost benefit of employee assistance programming. The actual studies cited above, and most other published reports, seem to support the validity of these projections and that EAPs are sound investments for most work organization. The average annual cost of a comprehensive in-house program is $20.38 per employee, with a range from $16 to $114—the latter being exceptionally high.[11] Most experts in the field agree, however, that the economic benefits are well worth the program costs. As one such expert put it, "EAPs are not cheap. But when measured against the likely costs involved in not having one, it appears to be one of the all-time bargains in the corporate world."[12]

PROGRAM COSTS VERSUS PROGRAM SAVINGS

In the absence of a very strong cost-benefit argument, many corporate managers might reject the concept of employee assistance programming. If it is not required by law, or does not show a net present value greater than the investment and operating costs, the EAP, or any other such proposal, will not go any further than the circular file. Capital investments, in some organizations, must show a quick and certain positive return.

The business of business and industry, many economists believe, is "to use its resources and engage in activities designed to increase its profits so long as it stays within the rules of the game."[13] The contention of such economists is that any investment activity including the acceptance of social responsibility by corporate officials undermines both the very foundation of our free society and the corporation's number one priority: to make as much money for the their stockholders as possible. This point of view reflects an attitude that social responsibilities are really governmental responsibilities and that the economic measure of performance is fundamental to business and industry.[14]

All arguments for social responsibility, corporate social responsiveness, and public policy notwithstanding, many business organizations would not have any program that could not express its benefits in economic terms. In order to win the approval of the organization's decision makers, some quantitative measure would have to assure the proposed project's economic viability. The program would have to project a dollar value.

While any organization could commission a research group to come in and conduct a unique study, such a study would be difficult and costly. Commissioning such a report would be a capital investment in and of itself. There are a number of research consultants capable of sophisticated and precise models that measure the economic efficiency of industrial alcoholism programs. To apply these models, however, several categories of economic data would be required: rehabilitation program costs, employee replacement costs averted, absenteeism cost reduction and reductions in costs of reduced productivity, sick leave, health insurance payments, and post-separation disability attributed to treatment.[15]

Some researchers in the field believe it is difficult, if not impossible, to use many of the recently developed, sophisticated cost-benefit-analysis techniques. Problems of measurement, conceptualization, and requirements for extensive data, and the "diffuseness of the resource allocation processes" in employee assistance programs contribute to that difficulty.[16] Such studies are simply too complicated and too costly. Yet, as illustrated above, several corporations have ignored these obstacles and have commissioned studies.

The same corporate manager who is not convinced by the existing pro-EAP literature and cost-benefit data is also not likely to be talked into a costly unique study. Since there are more corporations without employee assistance programs than with, it might be assumed that many corporate decision makers feel this way. As discussed in Chapter 3, while 86.8 percent of all companies with more than five thousand employees offer some form of employee counseling service, many employees are not covered by EAPs.[17] The majority of U.S. corporations, in fact, when including those with under five thousand employees, do not have employee assistance programs and do not offer services designed to address or reduce alcohol and/or drug-related job-performance problems.

The fact that so many organizations elect not to provide such services suggests that there may be an argument for both sides. The need for more sophisticated research/evaluation models to demonstrate an EAP's current and/or potential cost benefit is, in itself, evidence that not all programs in all work organizations will always prove cost effective. For one thing, the majority of workers in America work for small companies with a total employee population of less than 500. It might not be economically feasible to install an EAP in such a company or, in fact, in any company with an employee population of less than one thousand. This is especially true where the employee turnover is not significant. A program that reaches 5 percent of its population, for example, might get 50 referrals in the first year. After that, the referral rate would be reduced to a trickle. If the company's objective is to reduce the cost of alcohol- and drug-related job-performance problems, the cost of the program and treatment costs of the troubled employees could exceed the cost benefit in small organizations. As discussed in Chapter 17, subscribing to the services of an outside EAP contractor or forming a consortium with other small companies is a viable alternative to an in-house program. The costs of these alternatives should also be examined carefully to assure the desired cost-effective objective.

One cost variable frequently cited when enumerating the economic benefits of an EAP is the expense of training new employees. Discharging a troubled employee whose chemical dependency has progressed to the point where job performance is seriously impaired means hiring a replacement. Replacement costs, including training and adjustment time lost, could be significant. Skilled technicians, engineers, executives, airline pilots, and any number of other job categories, for example, could mean high replacement costs. But what about the other levels of employment? It could be cheaper to hire and train new employees than to rehabilitate present employees. This is especially true where the employee population is predominantly non-skilled or semi-skilled. A garment center seamstress who earns $4.25 per hour or a Wall Street messenger earning $3.75 per hour will cost their respective companies the same $6,000 to $18,000 for a 28-day stay at a private hospital that it would pay for one of its corporate executives.[18] There are, of course, less expensive rehabilitation alternatives but the point is that such variables determine whether or not an EAP is financially viable.

All of the variable costs averted have to be measured against the costs of program implementation and operation. Replacement costs, absenteeism costs, reduced productivity costs, health insurance payment costs, and other germane costs enter into the cost-benefit formula that determines the economic value, negative or positive, of the existing or planned EAP. If a company's actual or anticipated program costs are greater than program savings, then the rationale for installing or maintaining an EAP must be found elsewhere.

THE DOLLARS, SENSE, AND SUM OF IT ALL

The terms "cost benefit," "cost effectiveness," and "cost containment" entered the vocabulary of employee assistance programming early on. As noted in Chapter 3, the first programs were motivated to a great extent by economic concerns, and later EAPs began to express program value through cost-benefit analyses and cost-effectiveness studies. These measures of success have served as the impetus for the growth of employee assistance programming and, in combination with those benefits that are not easily quantifiable, provide a humanistic/cost-benefit package that appeals to both "rational" and "human relations" models of management. Those benefits that are not easily quantified are at least as important as those that are. Employees who feel good about themselves are likely to be more productive than those who do not. Similarly, employees who feel the organization is genuinely concerned about their health and welfare will tend to be loyal to that organization. While providing help for chemically dependent employees is important, most EAPs offer assistance on a wide range of problems. All personal problems adversely affect job performance, and helping troubled employees, whatever their problems are, is likely to improve job performance.

The value of having an employee assistance program can be expressed in many ways. Whatever methods or values are used to determine its viability, the ultimate benefactor must be the organization paying for the EAP. The following quotation expresses both its human and economic benefit:

> In all, it seems clear that more and more employers will assume responsibility for the rehabilitation of the troubled employee as the most constructive, humane and least costly path available. In doing so, the employer at best will be able to convert non-productive employees into productive ones and at least to cut short company losses attributed to long-term tolerance of the non-productive employee by identifying those employees, fulfilling company obligations to them with respect to rehabilitation and terminating the employees who cannot comply. In the long run, these policies will benefit employers as well as employees.[19]

NOTES

1. "McDonnell Douglas Corporation's EAP Produces HARD DATA," *The ALMACAN*, 19, No. 8 (August 1989): 18–26.

2. Louis Harris & Associates, "Trends in Use of Alcohol and Drugs 1989," New York City.

3. National Institute on Drug Abuse, "National Household Survey on Drug Abuse: Population estimates 1988," U.S. Department of Health and Human Services (Rockville, MD: 1989), 17.

4. Donald W. Myers, "Measuring EAP Cost Effectiveness: Results and Recommendations," *EAP Digest* (March/April 1984): 44.

5. Harrison M. Trice and Mona Schonbrunn, "A History of Job-Based Alcoholism Programs: 1900–1955," *Journal of Drug Issues*, ILR Reprint, Cornell University (Spring 1981): 174.

6. Norman R. Kurtz, Bradley Googins, and William C. Howard, "Measuring the Success of Occupational Alcoholism Programs," *Journal of Studies on Alcohol*, 45, No. 1 (New Brunswick, NJ : Center of Alcohol Studies, Rutgers University, January 1984): 33.

7. William S. Duncan, *The EAP Manual* (New York: National Council on Alcoholism, 1982), 6.

8. Walter Scanlon, "Trends in EAPs: Then and Now," *EAP Digest* (May/June 1983), 39.

9. "McDonnell Douglas Corporation's EAP Produces HARD DATA," *The ALMACAN*, 19, No. 8 (August 1989): 18–26.

10. "McDonnell Douglas Corporation, Employee Assistance Program Financial Offset Study 1985–1989," Bridgeton, MO, 1990, Alexander & Alexander Consulting Group.

11. Estimate for 1992 based on Anne Kiefhaber and Willis B. Goldbeck, "Industry's Response: A Survey of Employee Assistance Programs," in *Mental Wellness Programs for Employees*, ed. by Richard H. Egdahl and Diana Chapman Walsh (New York: Springer-Verlag, 1980), 25.

12. Marvin Grosswirth, "Stoned at the Office," *Datamation* (February 1983): 30.

13. George A. Steiner, John B. Miner and Edmond R. Gray, *Management Policy and Strategy* (New York: Macmillan, 1982), 81, 82.

14. Ibid.

15. J.M. Swint, M. Decker, and D. Lairson, "Economic Evaluation of Industrial Alcoholism Programs," *Journal of Studies on Alcoholism* 38, No. 9 (New Brunswick, NJ: Rutgers University, 1978): 1633–39.

16. Carl J. Schramm, "Evaluating Occupational Programs: Efficiency and Effectiveness," In *NIAAA Research Monograph-8/Occupational Alcoholism: A Review of Research Issues* (Washington, DC: Government Printing Office, 1982): 363–371.

17. Bureau of Labor Statistics, *The World Almanac* 1990 (New York: Pharos Books, 1990): 105.

18. Current rates based on room and board plus medical and physician's expenses (1991).

19. Janet Maleson Spencer, "The Developing Notion of Employer Responsibility for the Alcoholic, Drug-Addicted or Mentally Ill Employee: An Examination Under Federal and State Employment Statutes and Arbitration Decisions," *St. Johns Law Review*, 53, No. 4 (Summer 1979): 720.

8

Marketing the EAP: Employees Who Refer Themselves

THE EAP AS AN EMPLOYER-SPONSORED BENEFIT

The EAP can be described as an employer-sponsored benefit that provides employees and family members assistance with personal problems. In addition to helping employees who have become chemical dependent, the EAP may assess, refer, and counsel employees who are experiencing problems at home, having difficulty in relationships, needing social services, managing finances poorly, gambling heavily, needing legal advice, or simply in need of someone to talk with. Depending upon the design and scope of the EAP function, the program may either provide services in-house or refer to appropriate community resources for assistance and/or treatment.

In organizations with comprehensive EAPs capable of handling a variety of personal problems, the self-referral rate is likely to be considerably higher than those programs focusing only on chemical dependency. This is because employees needing help with other problems are more likely to voluntarily seek out the services of an EAP than those who are chemically dependent. There are several factors that contribute to this phenomenon. The first is that denial of the problem is characteristic in drug and alcohol abusers, with the abuser consciously or unconsciously not associating the substance with the emerging problems. Chemical dependency, therefore, is likely to progress to the point where other serious problems such as deteriorating job performance are evident. By this time the supervisor will have already referred the employee to the EAP. Second, rather than seeing alcohol or drug abuse as a problem, the troubled employee sees it as a solution to the problem. Voluntarily seeking help from the EAP would mean placing this "solution" in jeopardy. The third factor is that most other personal problems typically found in the workplace are of a short-term nature. Consequently, the supervisor will not have observed deteriorating job performance over a long period of time.[1] While there are exceptions to this observation, these employees will discover the EAP or seek outside help before a supervisory referral becomes necessary.

TRUST AND CONFIDENTIALITY

In discussing employee assistance programming and supervisory referrals, the word "confidentiality" is usually used in the legal sense. It is likely to be followed by other legal terms and phrases such as "release of information," "code of federal regulations," "patient rights," and so on. The alcohol- and drug-abusing patient may be protected under federal laws and state laws, and other troubled employees may be protected under provisions of federal privacy acts and local laws where applicable. These laws, statutes, regulations, and guidelines, when applicable, are intended to protect all patients, including employees using the services of the company EAP. Employees who are referred by supervisors as well as those who refer themselves are equally protected. Confidentiality, therefore, is assured whatever the employee's status may be. It should be noted, however, that explicit confidentiality concerns, in the legal sense, are governed by a final rule promulgated in 1987 for programs that provide "alcohol or drug diagnosis, treatment, or referral for treatment and which are federally assisted directly or indirectly." That rule was written primarily for the guidance of federally financed treatment programs, not private sector EAPs.[2] [References to "confidentiality" will appear throughout this book. Check the index for more information on this subject.]

"Confidential communication," as described by the American College Dictionary, is "a confidential statement made to a lawyer, doctor, or priest, or to one's husband or wife, privileged against disclosure." "Trust," however, is "the obligation or responsibility imposed on one in whom confidence or authority is placed." The point here is that "confidentiality" is mandated by law while "trust" is assigned by a person.

The person who voluntarily seeks help from an EAP, albeit confidentiality is guaranteed, must also be assured that the person from whom help is being sought can be trusted. This means competence as well as confidence, and an unquestioning belief in the integrity, strength, and ability of the person entrusted. The employee who is likely to seek out an EAP for help, whatever the problem may be, either already knows, or is hoping that the EAP professional can be trusted. The employee has either been assured by a fellow employee that the company EAP is reliable, or the EAP has successfully marketed its reliability and trustworthiness to the employee population. In either case the self-referred employee will approach the EAP professional somewhat cautiously, assessing the qualifications, credentials, and level of concern before making a personal investment.

In one of many cases following similar patterns, an employee telephoned my office and asked for information on alcoholism and what to do if a drinking problem seemed apparent. I talked with the employee for a short while and suggested a one-on-one counseling session to discuss the problem further, assuring the employee that confidentiality would be maintained. The caller rejected the offer, however, thanking me for the information and promising to call again if necessary. The employee declined to leave a name.

Some weeks later I received a call, once again, from the anonymous caller. The caller had thought about what we had discussed previously and concluded that there did seem to be symptoms of an alcohol problem present. The caller admitted to having a safety-sensitive position, adding that while drinking on the job was not his problem, a reputation as a "drunk" might jeopardize job security. I responded, once again, to specific questions about alcohol abuse and treatment options available, adding that a personal meeting would better lend itself to discussing these options further. The employee reminded me that I mentioned "confidentiality" during our previous telephone talk and asked me specific questions about this aspect of the program. After a few more minutes of talking the caller thanked me for my time, this time asking if it would be all right to call again in a few days. The caller, once again, declined to leave a name.

Two days later I received a third call from the same employee. This time the employee did not hesitate to give me a name, asked for an appointment to meet with me, and showed up promptly as scheduled. In our first meeting the employee continued to assess the program, exercising discretion and caution in both asking questions and providing answers. After the second session, however, the employee's uncertainty and caution had diminished and treatment planning became possible.

There is nothing dramatic about this case study. The point here, in fact, is to show the subtlety yet importance of establishing trust and emphasizing confidentiality. After the first telephone conversation the employee had enough information to choose any number of treatment options. These included several local treatment programs and self-help groups as alternatives to using the EAP directly. In talking with the employee and providing this information with no strings attached, the seed of trust had been planted. Through subsequent telephone talks and personal interviews the employee became satisfied that, whatever the organization's motives for providing such a service, the EAP practitioner showed both genuine concern and a pragmatic, professional approach to the employee's problem. This employee, incidentally, responded favorably to treatment and, at last count, had more than two years of continuous sobriety.

MARKETING TRUST AND COMPETENCE

Marketing is a human activity directed at satisfying needs and wants through exchange processes. *Exchange* is one of four ways in which a person can satisfy his or her needs. The other three are *self-production, coercion* and *supplication.* The exchange process assumes four conditions, and while any one of these conditions may also apply to any one of the other three means to satisfying a need or want, none but *exchange* require all four:

1. There are two parties.
2. Each party has something that could be of value to the other.
3. Each party is capable of communication and delivery.
4. Each party is free to accept or reject the offer.[3]

If these conditions exist, then there is a potential for exchange. Whether or not the exchange actually takes place depends on whether or not the two parties can find terms of exchange.

In the process of marketing employee assistance, the employee population is one party and the EAP is the other. While marketing principles and philosophies of business organizations generally serve to "create" a need and, ultimately, actualize a potential exchange between seller and purchaser, these principles are also applicable where profit is not the bottom line. Marketing in the true sense is being responsive to the needs of the people.[4] In attempting to reach a market where the marketing organization is not receiving direct payment for the services rendered, the success of the marketing efforts are often expressed in the number of people served. In this sense the marketing objective is truly "being responsive to the needs of the people," no strings (or cash) attached. Since the self-referred employee has not been referred by a supervisor, it could be assumed that job performance is acceptable. In actuality, however, a troubled employee who receives help will do a better job no matter how he got to the EAP.

Marketing the EAP is different from marketing a detergent or a soft drink. Unlike business marketing, the promotion of an EAP is closer to social marketing. It employs a change technology rather than a response technology, that is, getting people to stop doing something they want to continue to do. It is getting them to stop smoking, stop drinking, or stop using drugs.[5] While it can be argued that they *do* want to get help with their problems, this does not necessarily mean they want to give up whatever is causing their problems. A marketing strategy targeted to the person beginning to drink too much must provide the right message if a response is to be expected. A poster that states "We Help Alcoholics" is not, obviously, the right message.

Marketing an EAP is an integration of many separate functions: selling, distribution, advertising, research, development, and service. While training, not marketing, is important to the supervisory referral process, a well-articulated marketing strategy is essential to building a program that will yield a high percentage of self-referrals. Trust and competence must be conveyed to the employee population, and while word-of-mouth will serve this objective to some extent, an ongoing marketing effort is necessary to satisfy all EAP marketing objectives. This marketing effort is best understood when it is divided into functions:

Selling focuses on the needs of the seller while marketing focuses on the needs of the buyer. It is, nevertheless, an important function in marketing the EAP. If the EAP administrator is convinced that the program is a quality service, then "selling" the program to the employee population becomes an important marketing function.

Distribution is that function of marketing critical to using the EAP services. Since the EAP is not a product that can be delivered to the employee's desk or worksite, "distribution" means accessibility. The program location should not inhibit the chance of reaching any employee on any level. It should *never* be located in the personnel department. Ideally, the EAP should be in a remote location where employees can feel safe, preferably away from the organization's central offices.

Advertising is the method(s) selected to provide the messages that project competence, trustworthiness, and availability (with no strings attached). Media selection is the problem of finding the best way to deliver this message to the target audience. Since every employee is a potential client, the target audience is the entire employee population. The employee population, however, is segmented into many sub-groups: women, men, union, non-union, management, clerical, black, white, and so on. Groups are further divided by age, marital status, problem type, and so on. Advertising strategies should be designed to reach all segments of the population, such as, an article in the house organ about marital problems, a brochure targeted to the cocaine abuser, a presentation on all services available, a flier on help for employees with gambling problems, a film on women and drugs and how the EAP can help, a poster on helping the employee who may be experiencing a drinking problem, a white paper from the CEO restating the organization's policy on chemical dependency and/or other employee problems, or announcements of the EAP mailed directly to the home. The number of ways an EAP can advertise are limited only by the imagination of the program administrator. Whatever advertising vehicles are used, the message should always communicate that the EAP is a confidential service, and that confidentiality and trust will not be compromised under any circumstances!

Research is the function that allows the program to learn from its experiences and shape its services to the employees' needs. Problem areas can be identified by reviewing where the self-referred employees are coming from, what kinds of problems they are coming with, how they learned about the program, what has happened since they came for help, how they were treated by the community program they were referred to, and any other information relevant to program development. This function also measures the effectiveness of advertising in terms of reach, frequency, and impact of the message delivered. The absence of self-referred employees from any particular department, division, or worksite within the organization will alert the EAP administrator to a possible marketing deficiency.

Development follows research and can mean either developing new markets or developing new services. In learning about those "markets" within the organization which are not being reached by the EAP, marketing strategies could be developed to increase activity. The physical location of the EAP may not be good, or the language in the literature may be masculine and alienate women, or the brochures may be directed at front-line employees and missing management personnel, and so on. Perhaps a woman, minority person, recovering alcoholic, or drug abuser should be added to the EAP staff to reach hard-to-reach segments of the organization. The EAP may need to expand its services to reach a broader segment of the employee population, or it may have to market existing services more aggressively to encourage employees to use the program. Whatever action is taken, the objective of *development* is to reach all those troubled employees which the EAP is potentially capable of helping.

Service is the essence of employee assistance programming. In marketing language the EAP is called "a pure service" because there are no tangible goods exchanged.[6] Since the EAP's product is service, the service must be professional, accessible, and consistent. It is the EAP's responsibility to follow up on all employees who make contact, to determine whether or not continued assistance is necessary. Marketing an EAP is like marketing a service warranty without the goods. The EAP maintains credibility only as long as it is responsive to the needs of the employee population. It should never promise a service that it cannot deliver.

Marketing the EAP is a management function that needs the support of management to be effective. Strategic and tactical planning that facilitates program objectives are necessary, such as, literature, print media, education series, and films. Most important, the marketing plan should include a realistic budget that reflects the program's objectives in economic terms.

While program awareness and program visibility are important in generating supervisory and union referrals, they are especially important in generating self-referrals. A program is not successfully implemented until it has been satisfactorily marketed within the organization.[7] And marketing to the troubled employee who has not yet exhibited related job-performance problems is an ongoing responsibility of the EAP. A planned marketing effort to target this population will certainly show positive results. An acronym that accurately reflects the process is "AIDA": Getting the employee's *attention*; developing the employee's *interest*; creating a *desire* within the employee to resolve the problem; and giving the employee an opportunity to take *action*.

ARE SELF-REFERRALS REALLY SELF-REFERRALS?

Sometimes yes, sometimes no. A constructive confrontation conducted by a supervisor will often end on the note, "I suggest you get whatever help you need to bring your job performance up to par." Or the supervisor might recommend that the employee contact the company EAP. Or the employee may be under fire and make what he or she perceives to be a last-ditch effort to hold on to the job. While the EAP may carry this type of case as a self-referral, the factors motivating the employee are the same as those found in the supervisory referral model. The missing step is that the supervisor did not contact the EAP directly or require the employee to contact the EAP as a condition of continued employment. (Employees who are in safety-sensitive positions and are charged with drinking or using drugs while on duty are often required to accept treatment as a condition of continued employment.) The self-referred employee who has been told to "bring performance up to par" might be asked by the counselor what precipitated the EAP contact, or whether or not there have been problems on the job. But in most cases supervisory pressure will be denied and a different picture will be presented than that which eventually emerges. Like the employee who is referred for counseling by the medical department because of a swollen liver, or the union member who is advised to seek help by the shop steward, this type of case might be classified as a "soft referral" rather than a supervisory or self-referral. Progressive disciplinary procedures in some organizations require an "intervention interview" followed by a "warning interview" if job performance does not improve. This type of self-referral is often generated by the intervention interview.

A peer referral might be considered either a soft referral or a self-referral. While many organizations have EAPs with a peer-referral rather than a supervisory-referral design, an informal peer-referral network can serve the same objective: to get help for the troubled employee at the earliest possible stage. Camaraderie, mutual concern, and care are as much a part of the world of work as supervision, performance, and accountability. Both can work toward assisting the troubled worker.[8] The lines that separate the soft referral from the self-referral from the supervisory referral can be very thin. The notion of self-referral, nevertheless, allows the EAP to present itself as the employees' ally, and encourages employees to present themselves as responsible adults rather than people whose behavior is offensive and must be regulated.[9] The influences motivating the employee to seek help might be as obvious as poor job performance or as nebulous as not feeling good about oneself. Indeed, employees do not simply get up one morning and decide to go to the EAP; their decisions are made as a result of socialization and interactions with other people.[10] Whatever influences precipitate the employee's decision to seek help, the EAP must present itself as a professional, confidential, and competent function of the organization to assure that employees who might refer themselves do indeed refer themselves.

NOTES

1. Lewis F. Presnall, *Occupational Counseling and Referral Systems* (Salt Lake City: Utah Alcoholism Foundation, 1981), 187.

2. Richard Bickerton, MS, CEAP, "The Right To Privacy, The Need To Know: Are They Natural Enemies?," *Exchange*, EAP Association, Inc. (Arlington, VA, March 1990), 42.

3. Philip Kotler, *Marketing Management*, 4th ed. (Englewood Cliffs, NJ: Prentice-Hall, 1980), 19.

4. Robin E. MacStravic, *Marketing Health Care* (Germantown, MD: Aspen Systems, 1977), 7.

5. Walter F. Scanlon, "Non-Business Marketing Becomes Required Strategy," *Fund Raising Management* (August 1983): 48.

6. Kotler, *Marketing,* 374.

7. James L. Francek, "Marketing an EAP For Success," In *Human Resources Management Handbook/Principles and Practice of Employee Assistance Programs,* edited by Samuel H. Klarreich, James L. Francek, and C. Eugene Moore (New York: Praeger, 1985), 28.

8. Daniel J. Molloy, "Peer Referral: A Programmatic and Administrative Review," In *Human Resources Management Handbook/Principles and Practice of Employee Assistance Programs,* edited by Samuel H. Klarreich, James L. Francek and C. Eugene Moore (New York: Praeger, 1985), 108.

9. William J. Sonnenstuhl, "Understanding EAP Self-Referral: Toward a Social Network Approach," Contemporary Drug Problems, reprinted by Federal Legal Publications (1984), 288.

10. Ibid., 289.

9

Marketing Treatment: The Business of Recovery

THE COST OF TREATING THE CHEMICALLY DEPENDENT EMPLOYEE

Treating a chemically dependent employee costs as much as the purchase of a new Buick. Every time a residential treatment program admits a patient, it has, in effect, closed a deal tantamount to selling a mid-sized American car. The price tag for a 28-day stay in a typical chemical-dependency treatment program is $9,800. Some programs cost as much as $30,000 while others start at $5,000. Hospital-based programs usually cost more while free-standing programs are likely to cost less.

Whether an employer is referring an employee to a hospital-based program or a free-standing program, chemical-dependency treatment is a "big ticket" item. According to the Triangle Research Institute, industry invests more than $17 billion annually into the treatment of its chemically dependent employees.[1] A. Foster Higgins & Company, a New York–based benefit consulting firm, reports in its 1988 Health Care Benefits Survey that employers spent more than $36 billion for the treatment of mental illness.[2] Chemical dependency treatment may account for as much as 50 percent of this total. Giant corporations spend tens of millions of dollars for the treatment of chemically dependent employees and their family members. Even organizations considered to be small by Fortune 500 standards frequently spend millions of dollars for treatment services.

The methods by which treatment programs are paid may vary, but ultimately, the referring organization pays the bill. Self-insured employers and union trust funds pay directly while others may pay the form of premiums to their insurance carriers. (See Chapter 6 for more on this subject.)

WHERE THE REFERRALS COME FROM

A labor union with 15,000 members could make 125 referrals to residential rehabilitation programs in any given year through its member assistance program. Business corporations with as many employees may refer more or less, depending upon the promotional efforts of their employee assistance program and the constraints imposed by managed care. Based on a daily rate of $350 or a 28-day stay costing $9,800, a referral source sending 125 persons annually to residential rehabilitation treatment programs will pay about $1,225,000 for such services.

Of the 124 million workers in the United States, it is estimated that 19 percent—24 million people—have access to employee/member assistance programs.[3, 4] Using a conservative estimate that 5 percent of these employees are chemically dependent, there are a potential 1.2 million candidates for treatment. And this is only one source that treatment programs market their services to! Treatment programs also generate patients through direct advertising to the consumer. This may include radio and television commercials, yellow pages advertising public relations, and so on. Patient alumni word-of-mouth is one of the most important sources of referral for programs that have been in operation for a long time.

There are 2,820 private (including voluntary and proprietary) inpatient facilities competing for patients including rehabilitation programs, halfway houses, and detoxification units. There are also 2,572 outpatient programs with the same idea.[5] While inpatient and outpatient treatment programs assume different marketing positions, the targeted market is, nevertheless, the same: persons whose use of alcohol or other drugs is making their lives unmanageable.

The per-diem rate for detoxification is usually higher than that for residential rehabilitation, because it is a medical service requiring physicians and nurses. A rate of $400 per day is not unusual and many hospitals bill at $1,000 per day. Outpatient rehabilitation treatment programs charge anywhere from $3,000 to $7,000 for treatment. This covers a structured, intensive, non-residential, four- to six-month program.

HIGH FEES DO (NOT) A PROFIT MAKE

Chemical dependency treatment is, relatively speaking, a low-tech service. It does not require magnetic resonance imaging, respirators, CAT scans, or genetically engineered medications. Detoxification requires medical and nursing supervision and dual diagnosed patients (those with underlying psychiatric problems) may require psychiatric supervision, but the typical alcohol or drug abuser in treatment responds favorably to a low-cost integrated treatment approach. This might include group and individual counseling, chemical dependency education, recreation and nutrition supervision, and, most importantly, twelve-step program involvement. Chemical dependency treatment program design does not require vast expenditures. While salaries for experienced treatment professionals are beginning to reach a respectable income level, they still earn a fraction of what qualified professionals in other fields earn. As for twelve-step programs, they are free.

Program location and the cost of building, restoring, leasing, or renting a program site will vary from program to program. This cost, in addition to personnel costs, food costs (inpatient programs), operating costs, marketing costs, interest payments, taxes, and so on, determine the total cost of operating a facility. A facility in New York City, Chicago, or Los Angeles is likely to be more costly to operate than one in Sandy Hook, Spring Lake, or Belmont. Real estate, personnel expenses, and taxes are likely to cost more in major cities. These differences notwithstanding, the break-even point in the treatment of chemical dependency is relatively low. While outpatient programs are on the low end of the scale in terms of profit margin, residential rehabilitation programs can realize substantial earnings *if* they reach their break-even point. This is a big "if" that determines a facility's investment in marketing.

Using a 120–bed residential treatment program located in middle America as an example, the break-even point may come with a census as low as thirty-six. One such site located in a remote but accessible area was purchased to develop into a residential chemical dependency treatment program. It was a turn-of-the-century mansion restored to its original condition. Extravagance was not spared in developing this program, attending to such details as flagstone walks, fountains, gazebos, and formal gardens. In addition to the mansion, the program site included a playhouse, indoor swimming pool, tennis courts, separate residence facilities, and a medical detoxification unit. All of this sat on 45 acres of property.

If this 120–bed facility managed to maintain a census of thirty-six, it could meet all operating expenses. These thirty-six patients, billed at $350 each, would result in gross revenues of $12,600 per day. If successful at collecting 80 percent of its billing rate, its accounts receivable would be $10,080 per day. Assuming total operating expenses of $10,000 to $15,000 per day (the variable being additional cost for each patient over thirty-six patients), the program breaks even with $80 to spare ($10,000 operating v. $10,080 revenue).

If this program managed to fill all 120 beds, its gross income would be $33,600 per day (80 percent of $42,000 billed). With operating expenses at $15,000 per day, pre-tax earnings would be $18,600 per day ($15,000 v. $33,600). This is a pre-tax profit of 124 percent!

With incentives like this, is it any wonder that chemical dependency treatment is a competitive business? In all fairness, however, this 124 percent does not take into consideration a marketing budget. But even if we add another $3,000 per day to cover this expense, the pre-tax profit would be 87 percent. If the facility is operating as a not-for-profit franchise, its taxes are nominal or nonexistent.

Chemical-dependency treatment facilities, whatever their modality, are in serious competition with each other. At $2,000 for five days of detoxification and $7,000 for six months of intensive outpatient treatment and $9,800 for one month of residential treatment, both hospital-based and free-standing facilities are looking for their share of the business. Not only are they "looking" for the business, they are aggressively marketing their facilities to anyone who is in a position to make a referral. These referral sources include business organizations, labor unions, governmental agencies, and their respective employee assistance and member assistance programs. It also includes membership organizations, hospitals, other treatment service providers, and the general public.

PUBLIC, VOLUNTARY, PROPRIETARY: THE DIFFERENCES

Marketing alcohol- and drug-abuse treatment services is a concept that evolved over the past decade. At the start of the 1990s residential treatment programs positioned themselves against the threat of managed care and the growing trend toward using outpatient treatment programs. All programs market their services to some extent, but only voluntary and proprietary programs (both private: not-for-profit and for-profit, respectively) market as businesses of a different kind might. Treatment programs qualify under one of three different auspices: public, voluntary, or proprietary. Treatment in public programs is paid for through tax dollars, while voluntary programs accept private insurance and receive private donations. Proprietary programs accept private insurance.

All three groups are likely to have self-pay rates and could be eligible for Medicaid and Medicare. A public program is not-for-profit by virtue of its governmental auspices, voluntary programs are not-for-profit by application (Section 501(c)(3)), and proprietary programs operate as any private business would—for profit. Both voluntary and proprietary programs are entrepreneurial and market their services in the same way. Public programs market their services minimally through advertising and promotion materials. Because they exist to satisfy existing public need, theoretically, there is no need to market their services.

Voluntary program status has both financial advantages and disadvantages. Unlike the proprietary programs, earnings must be used for salaries, operating expenses, and program development. Revenues cannot leave the voluntary corporation in the form of profit. But, because of its not-for profit status, the voluntary program is entitled to certain federal and state tax breaks. Proprietary programs are often critical of this financial advantage in that tax exemption is a form of government funding. Both sectors compete for the same business, but voluntaries have a marketing edge in that tax advantages and private donations provide a financial cushion that proprietary programs do not have.

Because marketing is a discipline traditionally associated with business and profit, some treatment programs are not comfortable with the word "marketing." (Treatment is traditionally associated with serving and helping.) Euphemisms such as "community relations" or "industrial relations" are often substituted for "marketing." Whatever they call it, all treatment programs market their services. Those that do not are not likely to stay in business.

In the business of chemical dependency treatment, the word "marketing" is often used to describe what is, in fact, personal marketing (selling). While personal marketing is a function of marketing, marketing is actually an integration of many separate functions. Four of these functions, sometimes referred to as the communications mix, are personal marketing, advertising, marketing promotion, and public relations. Related marketing functions are pricing the service, places of distribution, product or program development (including research), and customer service.

MARKETING: WHAT IT IS

Marketing is a systematic approach directed at satisfying needs and wants through an exchange process. Treatment programs are in an exchange relationship with referral sources. Each has a need to be satisfied. In simple terms, treatment and service is exchanged for money. While there are other ways to express this relationship in more humanistic terms, the objective of marketing is to generate revenue in the form of referrals. The care provided, we assume, will always be of the highest quality.

The communications mix for one program may be different from that of the next. Some programs put most of their marketing budget into advertising and marketing promotion. Television and radio commercials, and trade and consumer print advertising are sometimes the media of choice. Slick four-color brochures and magazine quality newsletters are not uncommon, and novelty logo items such as coffee mugs and pens are commonplace. A few programs even have public relations practitioners on staff and advertising agencies developing costly media campaigns.

PERSONAL MARKETING FOR A COMPETITIVE EDGE

Whatever the communications mix may be, more and more programs are relying on personal marketing in order to stay competitive. A survey of selected east coast treatment programs show that all had personal marketing in their communications mix. The programs surveyed ranged in the number of treatment beds from thirty-six to 141, and personal marketers from three to eight.[6] Several major corporations operating or managing treatment facilities are firmly committed to personal marketing. One such organization has a small army of personal marketers, as many as eighty, operating out of more than twenty regional offices. With a total of 790 beds, the ratio of treatment beds to personal marketers in this organization is about 10:1! That is, each personal marketer is responsible for keeping up to ten beds filled.

A treatment facility in Tennessee with ninety-two beds has ten personal marketers. Not only does it have ten marketers, it also receives referrals through its corporate marketing efforts. The budget for personal marketing alone, not including advertising, marketing promotion, and public relations expenses, is $750,000. Their total marketing budget is about $1.25 million. The beds to marketers ratio here is about 9:1. To look at the importance placed on personal marketing in another way, each bed in this facility costs between $8,000 and $13,500 annually to market ($750,000 ÷ 92 = $8,152, or $1,250,000 ÷ 92 = $13,586).

Another health care corporation managing thirteen chemical dependency hospitals in the southeast has forty-four personal marketers. Its bed to marketer ratio is approximately 10:1. This organization has three to four personal marketers at each of their facilities and a marketing budget that well exceeds $5 million for just its marketing communications mix.

EVERYONE IS A PERSONAL MARKETER

Marketing, as discussed above, means much more than just selling. Personal marketing (selling) is only one part of the communications mix. It is an important part in the field of chemical dependency treatment, but it is one of many parts that must come together in an orchestrated fashion. Marketing, in fact, is a management function of the organization. It is an integrated function that involves the entire treatment program. Every person who works for a treatment program represents that program. From the receptionist who answers the telephone (on the first ring, one hopes), to the counselor who communicates with the referral sources, to the admissions worker, to the business office staff members—all are critical to the marketing effort. Each person in the organization delivers a message that says more (for better or for worse) about the organization than any one personal marketer can. If a referring organization does not get the service expected, all the personal marketing in the world cannot convince it that it did. While quality care is essential, convenience and effective communications are necessary to ensure repeat business.

It is here, unfortunately, that many treatment programs fail in their marketing efforts. A treatment program's quality of care may be exemplary, but its service may range from marginal to poor. This is especially true of programs that have enjoyed financial success in less competitive times, and perhaps may have had waiting lists in the past. This is not to say that the treatment program treats its referral sources in a shoddy or non-businesslike manner. Rather, it may not yet realize the need to compete in the changing environment.

Marketing in the business world is sometimes referred to as "demand management." Some programs are not hearing the demands being made. Referral sources expect both continuing care and family program counseling to be included in the treatment package. Rehabilitation programs must provide transportation to the facility and submit treatment reports in a timely manner. Whatever the demand is, the treatment program must be responsive to it. This assumes, of course, that treatment is not compromised in any way. To use an economics term, the increasing competitiveness of chemical dependency treatment has created a "price elasticity of demand." Simply stated, referral sources are looking for the most value in their treatment dollar expenditures. If they don't get it from one program, they will find another. Over a one-year period, more than one hundred residential programs nationwide have gone out of business. The National Association of Addiction Treatment Providers reports that census is at an all-time low. From 80 percent three years ago, some programs are operating at 50 percent of capacity. Twenty-eight- to thirty-day stays are a thing of the past. The average inpatient stay is now seventeen to twenty-one days.[7] Residential rehabilitation programs were the treatment of choice in the 1980s, but outpatient modalities are gaining ground in the 1990s. In the absence of hard data supporting the success of one modality over the other, referral sources are likely to look more closely at cost and service. We are not likely to see waiting lists for residential treatment in private facilities in the 1990s.

MARKETING CLIENT SERVICE

Not all established treatment programs provide bad customer service and not all new treatment programs provide great customer service. New programs, in fact, are often built on old tradition, and old tradition has it that health care is a service, not a business. The reasoning here comes from the public auspices model of health care where treatment services existed to help those in need. Those in need of health care would find the service through public information; therefore, the need to market the service did not exist. Many programs are also operating under the influencing philosophy of Alcoholics Anonymous—"a program of attraction not promotion."

In staffing a new facility, a search for the best treatment professionals usually means recruiting from existing programs. Many of these programs will be in the public sectors, where salaries are usually lower and the concept of "profit" does not exist. This is not to say that professionals recruited from public sector programs will not understand the importance of customer service and marketing. But collectively, a program staff not recruited from the voluntary or proprietary sectors will need training. Inservice training can be effective but such an initiative must be established before the program admits its first patient. In fact, it should be established before the program hires its first staff member. Marketing and management are inseparable functions of the organization. A chemical dependency treatment program must be market focused if it is to survive in today's competitive environment.

In one respect, the chemical dependency treatment program must be more cognizant of the importance of marketing, specifically customer relations, than most other types of business. It must satisfy the needs and wants of two clients—the patient and the referral source. While most consumer products or services are used by the purchaser, chemical dependency treatment is an exception. Excluding a small percentage of individuals who pay cash for their own treatment, a third party is involved. That third party is the insurance carrier, the managed care reviewer (when applicable), and the referral source. Assuming that the referral source manages the case through treatment, this is the client whose demands must be satisfied if repeat business is to be expected. Employee/member-assistance program counselors, health-care fund managers, and other referral sources decide where individuals will be treated and their decisions are based on three factors. First, is the quality of care good? Second, is the cost acceptable? And last, but not least, will this treatment resource make their job easier and more pleasant? While a referral source's needs may vary somewhat, desirable basic requirements can be summed up as follows:

1. Treatment program that meets patients' needs
2. Competitive treatment cost
3. Professional and efficient admission procedure
4. Timely patient transportation to the facility
5. Progress reports consistent with referral source's requirements
6. Family involvement in treatment process
7. Patient transportation from facility upon discharge
8. Continuing care planning, case management, and timely progress reports

As easy as it seems to satisfy these requirements, few treatment programs do so consistently. Starting with number one, all programs have some form of exclusionary criteria. As an EAP coordinator, I had an employee who was on 60 milligrams of methadone and was physically handicapped. Finding a program that could meet this patient's needs was not an easy task. When I finally found a program that would accept him, I was happy to waive my other requirements just to get him in. The limited number of resources available for this type of case left me no choice.

That case was, admittedly, not a typical chemical-dependency case. Yet, even attempting to refer less complicated cases often became a chore. Not because the treatment program did not provide what they considered to be good treatment, but rather because it did not fully understand the concept of good customer service. They did not understand marketing as defined earlier in this chapter: a systematic approach directed at satisfying needs and wants through an exchange process. This fact is borne out in interviewing other employee/member assistance program directors. In negotiating with treatment programs around the eight requirements listed above, referral sources concurred that while most of the programs agreed to some, if not all, of these or similar requirements, few programs consistently delivered what they had promised. Typical problems included not being able to refer an employee who may have had a history of, albeit minor, psychiatric or medical problems. Overbilling or billing for "ancillary" services not in the original agreement occurs frequently. Admission's offices are often not responsive to referral source's needs such as prompt approval for admission. While many programs boast of 24–hour, seven-day admissions policy, few programs actually admitted during fringe times. Patient transportation to and from the facility was often a problem. Cars were often late and sometimes did not show at all. Progress reports, discharge summaries, and consistent feedback to the referral sources was often an ongoing problem. Some EAPs reported instances where their employees were discharged from treatment facilities without notifying the EAP counselor.

"ENTERTAINMENT" NOT THE ANSWER

While employee assistance and member assistance programs continue to compromise their service demands in the interest of serving their troubled employees, the 1990s will see some changes. Chemical-dependency treatment is becoming more competitive and treatment programs are positioning to ensure their share of the market. With managed care and outpatient programs cutting into inpatient admissions and profits, residential rehabilitation programs must make changes. They realize that staying in business means more than providing good treatment. It means satisfying all the client's needs and wants. Unfortunately, some treatment programs are looking for the easy way out. Rather than tightening up and guaranteeing good service, they are putting their marketing dollars into personal marketing and "entertainment." Wining and dining and weekend jaunts to lush and plush getaways are being offered by some programs. Even more unfortunate is the fact that some EAPs are compromising their program needs and wants for their own personal needs and wants. The host treatment program always includes a tour of their facility as part of the "marketing" excursion, of course. But in a profession where such entertainment practices are not de rigueur, such opportunities may inhibit the ability to make sound treatment and service choices.

While chemical-dependency treatment is no less of a business than leasing fleets of automobiles to major corporations, the rules of the game are different. The health care profession is bound by codes of ethics and professional codes of behavior. Some behavior is so clearly unethical and unacceptable it requires no discussion. Other actions lie

in the grey areas where rationalization can make questionable practices seem all right if not examined too closely. Sometimes these are,
indeed, all right when seen in full context.[8] It is this grey area that the
profession must concern itself with. All professionals, in fact, and all
public servants can easily find themselves in this grey area. And the
perception of impropriety is not very different from acts of impropriety. On June 4, 1987, *The Washington Post* reported that congres-
sional Representative Mario Biaggi was indicted in the Wedtech case
on violating anti-racketeering laws.[9] While this was one of several
criminial acts of impropriety that Biaggi was charged with, the one
that first got the public's attention was his accepting a free vacation.
In the business of chemical-dependency treatment, anything more
than a one-day facility visit, especially when that facility is located in
a resort-like environment, could be perceived as a free vacation.

THE UNCONDITIONAL SERVICE GUARANTEE

As discussed earlier in this chapter, the key to success in the chemical-dependency treatment business is the management of treatment
and service from a marketing perspective. And the most effective way
to ensure repeat business is to ensure client satisfaction. A satisfied client has no reason to take his business elsewhere. An
employee/member assistance program that receives both good treatment and service from a few selected treatment programs is likely to
continue to refer to those programs. This is not to say that these
relationships will be problem-free, but that problems will be resolved
expeditiously. An unconditional service guarantee (USG) may, in fact,
be the most effective way to establish exemplary service.

Some treatment program managers might argue that, by definition,
services simply cannot be guaranteed; that services are generally
delivered by human beings who are less predictable than machines.
Furthermore, services are usually produced at the same time they are
consumed, so how can something that no longer exists be guaranteed?
Unlike a camera, which can be sent back to the factory for repairs, a
bad service experience cannot be repaired.

In an article on the concept of the USG, the *Harvard Business Review*
argues that not only is it a good idea, but that committing to error-free
service can help a company provide it. If designed and implemented
properly, it enables one to get control over the organization. It
provides the organization with clear goals, information, and data
needed to continue to improve on service.[10]

A USG provides an opportunity to monitor important service
responsibilities, document reports of failure, and use these data to

eliminate such problems. The best way to guarantee service is to provide the referral source, in writing, with what can be expected in terms of service. The referral source should be asked *please* to report any inconsistency in service immediately to a specific person within the organization, such as the regional marketing director. Thirty days after the patient is discharged from the treatment program, the referral source should be contacted and asked, specifically, whether each and every one of these services were provided on time. This information should be logged and analyzed. Where failures have occurred, the USG is invoked.

Whatever compensation the treatment program elects to provide when service does not meet expectation is a matter for each facility to decide, but it should be meaningful. A scholarship, to be used when needed, might be considered. Some program administrators might feel that is a high price to pay for being a half-hour late, but a strong service guarantee will certainly ensure repeat referrals and establish a client service attitude throughout the treatment organization.

MAXIMIZING MARKETING IMPACT

An unconditional service guarantee has five qualifiers: First, it is unconditional, that is, if the terms of the USG have been violated, no matter the excuse, the referral source is compensated. Second, it should be easy to understand and communicate. Third, the compensation or the referral's response must be meaningful. Fourth, it must be easy and painless to invoke; invoking the USG should be encouraged and treatment center response should be gracious. Fifth, the compensation should be easy to collect.

The odds of gaining powerful marketing impact from a service guarantee are in your favor when one or more of the following conditions exist:

The price of service is high. A botched shoeshine is no big deal. Poor service or poor treatment at a cost of $3,000 to $30,000 is.

The client's ego is on the line. No one likes to admit to this one, but everyone likes to be treated like they are special.

The client's expertise with the service is low. When in doubt about a service, the client will usually choose a treatment program that he/she can trust. A USG provides that trust.

The negative consequences of service failure are high. The negative consequences of treatment, whatever they are, are almost always high.

The industry has a bad image for service quality. While most referral sources may agree that service is "adequate," many are not as kind.

The organization depends on frequent client purchases. A treatment program that loses its referral source after one or two referrals will be out of the treatment business within six months.

The organization's business is affected deeply by word of mouth. Treatment programs rely on word of mouth. Negative comments will put a facility out of business in no time.[11]

Obviously, the business of chemical-dependency treatment meets many of the above criteria. Service failure, word-of-mouth influences, the need for repeat business, and the high cost of treatment directly apply. As we said at the opening of this chapter, treating a chemically dependent person can cost as much as the purchase of a new Buick. This alone qualifies a treatment program as an organization that would benefit from a USG.

Major service violations such as discharging patients without notice will be reported by most EAP practioners. Late pickups, untimely feedback, and less-than-professional discharge summaries, however, are noted but not always brought to the treatment program's attention. Referral sources are not likely to take the time to lodge such complaints. They will, however, use that facility less frequently and, eventually, not at all. Personal experience at the moment of service delivery determines every client's perception of the organization. If the quality of service fails to meet the client's expectations, then the organization's other efforts become less than important.[12] A facility may do exemplary clinical work, but if the service is not good, it will not get referrals. The exchange relationship between the treatment program and the referral source is only as solid as the quality of care *and* service provided. A USG facilitates this objective.

Marketing is a high-order integration of many separate functions. It is not any one activity of the organization; it is many activities involving every employee. Each activity shares equal importance. The first and most important task of the treatment facility is to develop a clinically sound program with an uncompromising commitment to long-term recovery for the chemically dependent person. This objective applies whether the patient is in a detoxification unit, residential rehabilitation program, or outpatient clinic. Family involvement, continuing care, and twelve-step program involvement are almost always part of the recovery process.

While stating the obvious takes on the tone of preaching to the choir, these basic, common-sense concepts are often overlooked in both marketing planning and operations management. Utilization review and quality assurance should be applied to both clinical and service functions of the organization. It is necessary to do a periodic audit to insure that the mission of the organization including its commitment to good service has not been compromised over time. Chemical dependency treatment is, for the most part, a dedicated field. Yet the adage of "When you're up to your hips in alligators, you forgot that your original mission was to clean out the swamp" applies here. The original commitment, within the context of the present environment, needs continuing assessment.

The communications mix, including personal marketing, advertising, marketing promotion, and public relations are essential in today's competitive marketplace. Not only must the treatment program be clinically sound, it must compete with all the rest of the clinically sound programs. Related marketing functions such as pricing the service, program location, program development, as well as research and customer service are critical to success and should be monitored. This is necessary if a treatment program is to stand out among the rest. Even those programs that have developed a reputation for being synonymous with good treatment are changing gears and repositioning to maintain their market share. With most residential programs operating at less than full census, and a growing number of facilities filing Chapter XI, the survivors will be the innovators who are dedicated to both client *and* clinical service.

NOTES

1. Research Triangle Institute, updated costs based on 1983 study, dated March 21, 1990.

2. Robin B. Weiner and Debra Siegel, "Managed Mental Health Care Issues and Strategies," *Benefits Quarterly*, 5, No. 3 (Third Quarter 1989): 21–31.

3. "Employer Investment in Employee Assistance Programs," The Employee Assistance Professionals Association, Arlington, VA, January 1990 (Photocopy).

4. U.S. Department of Labor, Bureau of Labor Statistics, Office of Employment and Unemployment Statistics, Division of Occupational and Administrative Statistics, "The Employment Situation," (Washington DC, USDL89–528, October 1989).

5. *National Drug and Alcoholism Treatment Unit Survey (NDATUS), 1987, Final Report*, National Institute on Drug Abuse, National Instutute on Alcohol Abuse and Alcoholism (Rockville, MD: DHHS Publication No. 89–1626, 1989), 18, 19. Note: Estimates based on projection of outpatient and inpatient against private for-profit and non-profit total units.

6. Study conducted by Bethany Associates, March 1990.

7. Kenneth H. Bacon, "Private Drug Abuse Treatment Centers Try to Adjust to Life in the Slow Lane," Statistics attributed to Michael Q. Ford, President, National Association of Addiction Treatment Providers (NAATP), *The Wall Street Journal*, July 23, 1990, B1.

8. LeClair Bissell, M.D. and James E. Royce, S.J., Ph.D., *Ethics for Addiction Professionals*, (Center City, MN: Hazelden, 1987), 54.

9. George Lardner, "Rep. Biaggi Indicted in Wedtech Case," *The Washington Post*, June 4, 1987, A3.

10. Christopher W.L. Hart, "The Power of Unconditional Service Guarantee," *Harvard Business Review*, July-August 1988, 54–62.

11. Ibid.

12. Kaset International, *Extraordinary Customer Relations* (Tampa: 1990), 1.

10

The Standards and the Structure

DEVELOPING THE EAP STANDARDS

The growth of employee assistance programming has produced a body of knowledge important to both program planners and managers. Research and experience in the field are the bases for formulating the standards and guidelines that are the foundation of any effective program. These standards apply to any form of EAP service including programs developed and staffed internally, consulting firms that contract with work organizations and/or labor unions, and organizations that join together in a consortium sharing a central EAP service.

These standards are also applicable to any size organization in any sector. Private corporations, large and small, labor unions, municipalities, law enforcement agencies, public organizations, professional groups and associations apply these guidelines in developing and operating their programs. Without the structure that these standards provide, the professional integrity of employee assistance programming in its present form would not have been possible.

The "Standards for Employee Alcoholism and/or Assistance Programs" were first developed in 1981. These standards were formulated by the Blue Ribbon Program Standards Committee, a group of leaders in the fields of employee assistance programming, personnel management, and labor relations. The committee was formed in a special meeting called by the National Council on Alcoholism (NCA), in which representatives from the federal government, organized labor, and the Association of Labor-Management Administrators and Consultants on Alcoholism (ALMACA) participated. (Note: In 1989 both NCA and ALMACA changed their names, to the National Council on Alcoholism and Drug Dependence (NCADD) and the Employee Assistance Professionals Association (EAPA), respectively.) Holding its first meeting in New York City on January 14, 1980, the committee took its first step in developing the first complete set of standards for employee alcoholism and/or assistance programs. These standards were divided into five major categories. They included (1) policy and procedure, (2) administrative functions, (3) education and training, (4) resources, and (5) evaluation.[1]

INTRODUCTION TO THE EAP STANDARDS

In 1988 ALMACA (EAPA) recognized the need for more detailed standards which reflect advancements in the EAP field. It appointed a Program Standards Committee to develop revised standards. In 1990 the revised EAP Standards were released. These new standards are organized and divided into six general areas: (1) design, (2) implementation, (3) management and administration, (4) direct services, (5) linkages, and (6) evaluation.[2]

The following pages contain these standards, excluding the "intent" of each standard. The complete document, including "intent", is available through the EAPA in Arlington, Virginia. Also available is "The Consumer Guide" for applying these standards. The purpose of the EAP standards is to:

Define the EAP field as a profession

Describe the scope of EAP services

Educate the community regarding EAP services

Suggest application of program standards, guidelines, and definitions

Serve the needs of the EAP membership[3]

THE STANDARDS

I. Definition

An employee assistance program (EAP) is a worksite-based program designed to assist in the identification and resolution of productivity problems associated with employees impaired by personal concerns including, but not limited to: health, marital, family, financial, alcohol, drug, legal, emotional, stress, or other personal concerns which may adversely affect employee job performance.

The specific core activities of EAPs include (1) expert consultation and training to appropriate persons in the identification and resolution of job-performance issues related to the aforementioned employee personal concerns and (2) confidential, appropriate and timely problem-assessment services; referrals for appropriate diagnosis, treatment, and assistance; the formation of linkages between workplace and community resources that provide such services; and follow-up services for employees who use those services.

II. Significance And Use

The objectives of an employee assistance program are these:

To serve the organization, its employees, and their families by providing a comprehensive system from which employees can obtain assistance addressing personal problems which may affect their work performance;

To serve as a resource for management and labor when they intervene with employees whose personal problems affect their job performance;

To effectively, efficiently, and professionally provide assessment, referral, and follow-up services for mental health, alcohol, and other drug-related problems in the workforce.

III. Program Design

A. Advisory Committee

There shall be an advisory function at a high level within the organization involving representatives of all segments of the work force.

B. Needs Assessment

Program design shall be based on an assessment of organizational and program needs as they relate to EAP utilization. The background information and organizational data to be factored into program design will include at least:

An organizational profile
Employee needs assessment
Surveys of supervisors and union representatives
A review of service delivery models

C. Service Delivery Systems

Employee assistance program services shall be delivered through a comprehensive, formal delivery system.

IV. Implementation

A. Policy Statement

The policy statement defines the EAP's relationship to the organization as well as describes the EAP as a confidential resource for the organization and its employees. Additionally, it shall state the scope of program services as well as the program's limitations. The policy statement shall include at least the following concepts:

The organization providing EAP services to its employees recognizes that a mentally and physically healthy employee is an organizational asset and that the availability of appropriate EAP services is beneficial to both labor and management.

Alcohol and other drug abuse, emotional, marital, family and other related problems affect job performance, employee health and quality of life. Such problems are treatable and are the legitimate concern of employers. Employees who experience these problems may be unable to function efficiently, effectively, and safely on the job.

Employees who need EAP services can voluntarily seek assistance, or they can be referred through constructive intervention. Job security, will not be jeopardized as a consequence of seeking EAP services, except where mandated by law. However, employees who use an EAP are expected to adhere to the job performance requirements of the employing organization.

All EAP records shall be kept strictly confidential and will not be noted in any official record or in the employee's personnel file. Information from the EAP may be released only with the written permission of the employee, or in response to the organizational EAP policy, or from a court or legal order (e.g., subpoena).

B. Implementation Plan

An implementation plan shall outline the actions needed to establish a fully functioning EAP and set fourth a timeline for their completion. The program implementation plan shall establish the EAP as a distinct service within the organization. The implementation plan shall cover the following:

1. Policy, procedures, and objectives
2. Logistics of service delivery including:
    Location resources, for space and staff
    Staffing ratio
3. An operations plan including:
    Program promotion and employee communications, orientation and education
    Training of supervisors and union representatives
    Review of health/mental health benefit coverage, and possible benefits redesign
    Identification of community resources
    Strategies for program integration
4. A management plan, including:
    Budget projections
    Record keeping
    Reporting procedures
    Quality assurance
    Liability coverage
5. An evaluation system including:
    Measurable objectives
    Appropriateness
    Efficiency
    Progress
    Outcomes

V. Management and Administration

A. Policy and Procedures

To achieve consistent and effective delivery of services, standardized policies and procedures for program administration and operation shall be developed in response to program objectives and organizational needs.

B. Staffing Levels

An adequate number of EAP professionals shall be available to achieve the stated goals and objectives of the program. Organizations that choose to contract for EAP services shall have at least one liaison person with formal responsibility for coordinating the delivery of services and monitoring contractor performance.

C. Staff Qualifications

Each EAP shall retain professionals qualified to perform their duties. Measures of qualifications should include evidence of specialized understanding alcohol and other drug problems and certification in employee assistance programming (CEAP). EAP professionals shall adhere to all government regulations regarding their scope of practice.

D. Community Networks

The EAP shall identify, foster, create, utilize, and evaluate community resources which provide the best quality care at the most reasonable cost.

E. Confidentiality

The EAP professional shall prepare and implement a confidentiality policy, consistent with all professional standards and ethics, and adhere to all other regulations that may apply to information in the position of the EAP. Disclosures will be specified by government guidelines and EAP policy and will be communicated to users of EAP services. The limits of the confidentiality policy shall be disclosed in writing to those who use the EAP.

F. Liability

All professionals shall have adequate professional and other appropriate liability coverage.

G. Ethics

EAP professionals shall adhere to the codes of ethics espoused by their professional organizations and by appropriate licensing or certifying bodies. Any actual or perceived conflict-of-interest among EAP professionals and service providers shall be avoided. Conflict-of-interest statements shall be filed when appropriate.

VI. Direct Services

EAPs deliver comprehensive quality services to three target groups: employees and covered family members, supervisory and union personnel, and the work organization as a whole.

A. Crisis Intervention

The EAP shall offer responsive intervention services for employees, covered family members, or the organization in acute crisis situations.

B. Assessment and Referral

EAP professionals, or an assessment service under contract to the organization, shall 1) conduct an assessment to identify employee or family member problems, 2) develop a plan of action, and 3) recommend or refer the individual(s) to an appropriate resource for problem resolution.

C. Short-Term Problem Resolution

EAP professionals shall determine when it may be appropriate to provide short-term problem resolution services, and when to make a referral to community resources. Long-term ongoing treatment is not part of the EAP model.

D. Progress Monitoring

The EAP shall review and monitor the progress of referrals. This shall include assisting in reintegration to the worksite if the employee is taken off the job for treatment.

E. Follow-Up

The EAP shall provide follow-up services to employees, covered family members, supervisory and union personnel, and the organization to monitor and support the progress of the resolution of personal problems and improvement of job performance.

F. Training

The EAP shall provide training for supervisory, management, and union personnel to give them an understanding of EAP objectives, procedures for referring employees experiencing job performance problems to the program, and the impact of the program on the organization.

1. Understanding EAP
   Impact of employee well-being on job performance
   Management of employees with problems
2. Consultation
   Recognition of an employee's need for assistance
   Methods of referral to the EAP

3. Program operation
    Relationship of EAP to personnel actions
    Confidentiality
    Reintegration
    Relationship to federally mandated drug testing and training

The EAP shall ask those who attend the training to provide written feedback after taking the course.

G. Supervisor/Union Consultation

EAP professionals shall provide individual consultation to supervisors and union representatives regarding the management and referral to the EAP of employees with job performance problems and other behavioral/medical problems.

H. Organization Consultation

EAPs shall be both proactive and responsive when organizational developments and events impact employee well-being and fall within the EAP professional's expertise.

I. Program Promotion

EAPs shall ensure the availability and use of promotional materials and activities which encourage the use of the program by supervisors, union representatives, peers, employees, and covered family members.

J. Education

Information about the EAP and its services shall be part of new employee orientation and ongoing employee education.

VII. Linkages

A. Internal Organizational Activities

The EAP shall be positioned at an organizational level where it can be most effective with linkage to the executive office. The EAP should establish working relationships with a variety of internal departments and committees, including:
    Human resources/personnel
    Benefits
    Safety
    Equal employment opportunity

Medical
Security
Risk management
Legal
Training department
Organizational development
Employee relations
Union

B. External Community Organizations and Resources

The EAP shall develop and maintain relationships with the external health care delivery system and other community resources which provide EAP-relevant services.

C. Professional Organizations

EAP professionals shall maintain and upgrade their knowledge through such activities as belonging to one or more organizations specifically designed for EAP professionals, such as the Employee Assistance Professionals Association (EAPA), attending training and/or continuing education programs, and maintaining regular, on-going contact with other employee assistance program professionals.

VIII. Evaluation

An EAP shall evaluate the appropriateness, effectiveness, and efficiency of its internal operations. Measurable objectives shall be stated for both process and outcome evaluation.[4]

EASNA STANDARDS

The Employee Assistance Society of North America (EASNA) has also developed a set of professional standards. EASNA's standards for Accreditation of Employee Assistance Programs are more similar than different from EAPA's standards. If a comparison could be made between the two, it appears that EASNA's standards, although incorporating the fundamental core technology (see page 111) of employee assistance programming to some extent, are more clinically focused. While the EAPA standards frequently refer to "work performance" and "problems of the workforce," EASNA standards refer to "behaviorally-linked health problems" that "have an adverse affect on the employer." EASNA standards are also more detailed around issues of staffing patterns, counseling hours, and clinical supervision. The differences between the two professional associations notwithstanding, each set of standards is an important contribution to the profession of employee assistance programming.

The general categories for the EASNA standards are as follows:

A. Administrative
B. Design and Implementation
C. Program Operations
D. Record Keeping
E. Confidentiality
F. Staffing
G. Staff Supervision
H. Staff Development
I. Managed Alcohol, Drug Abuse, and Mental Health Care in an EAP Setting
J. Evaluation
K. Research [5]

CORE TECHNOLOGY

The core technology is what sets employee assistance apart from other types of workplace counseling and coaching activities. Research has established eight dimensions of a well-managed employee assistance program. They are:

1. Constructive policy focusing the EAP on employees' alcohol and other substance abuse problems.
2. Provision of expert consultation to supervisors, managers, and union representatives on how to take appropriate steps in utilizing EAP policy and procedures.
3. Identification of employees' behavioral problems based on job performance issues.
4. Available and appropriate use of constructive confrontation to motivate employees.
5. Micro-linkages with counseling, treatment, and other community resources.
6. The creation and maintenance of macro-linkages between the work organization and such resources.
7. Expert consultation with worksite systems regarding organizational level policies relevant to health and related problems.
8. On-going evaluation of EAP utilization on the basis of work performance and benefit usage.[6]

NOTES

1. Blue Ribbon Program Standards Committee comprised of representatives from the Association of Labor-Management Administrators and Consultants on Alcoholism; the National Council on Alcoholism; the Occupational Program Consultants Association; the National Institute on Alcohol Abuse and Alcoholism; the U.S. Office of Personnel Management; and the AFL-CIO and other segments of organized labor, "Standards for Employee Alcoholism and/or Assistance Programs," New York: January 1981.

2. Standards for Employee Assistance Programs, *Exchange*, Employee Assistance Program Association, Inc. (Arlington, VA, October 1990 [special insert]).

3. Ibid.

4. Ibid.

5. EASNA Standards for Accreditation of Employee Assistance Programs, effective July 1, 1990, Employee Assistance Society of North America, Oak Park, IL (offset).

6. Attributed to Paul M. Roman and Terry C. Blum in "The Core Technology of 'Megabrush,'" John C. Erfurt, Andrea Foote, Max A. Heirich, Institute of Labor & Industrial Relations, The University of Michigan, September 1990.

11

Creating a Climate for EAP Utilization

ESTABLISHING THE EAP THROUGH POLICY

There are several factors that will influence and encourage the use of the EAP and contribute to the success of its efforts. Program credibility and management support are probably the two most important. Program credibility, in fact, is not possible without management support. The success of the program depends to a great degree on how it is perceived by the organization, and the organization's perception is shaped by the importance management places on the EAP function:

> The EAP should become an integral department of the corporation with the same opportunities for intra-corporate communication as other departments. Only in this way can the EAP perceive the pulse of the corporation and help it deal more effectively with its human resources.[1]

Program credibility, therefore, starts with an endorsement from management through the formulation and distribution of a corporate policy statement. Policy and procedure should reflect the organization's position on chemical dependency, affirming that alcoholism and drug abuse are serious health problems amenable to treatment. It should stress the importance of existing disciplinary procedures in program utilization, and should assure program participants that neither future employment nor career opportunities will be affected in any way. Confidentiality of all program records must, of course, be assured.

This is a start. A policy statement signed by the chief executive officer, and the union president if the program is a joint effort, is an essential first step in establishing program credibility with employees, supervisors, and union representatives. The troubled employee learns that chemical dependency is a health problem, the supervisor is introduced to the concept of "job jeopardy" as a tool to help the employee, and the union representative becomes aware that early intervention is the best strategy. The policy underscores the supervisor's role in getting the troubled employee to the EAP. A policy statement is a necessary prerequisite to an EAP's success, but it alone will not provide program credibility. Like a cornerstone in a building, it is the starting point from which the program is built.

ENGAGING BOTH EMPLOYEES AND SUPERVISORS

From the troubled employee's point of view, action speaks louder than words. Confidentiality, job-security, and the opportunity to get help must be demonstrated. Credibility is a growing process that comes as the employee population hears good things about the program. The employee must see the EAP as an employee service without a hidden agenda and the EAP counselor as a professional who can be trusted. The ethical standards established to guide the program must render it beyond reproach, and the integrity of the program must never be compromised.

From the point of view of the supervisor, "credibility" takes on a different meaning. The supervisor who refers a troubled employee expects the employee's job performance to improve. Where this is not happening, or where relapses occur, a dialogue between supervisor and program is important. This communication should never violate confidentiality requirements, but should serve to facilitate treatment and management objectives. As the supervisor begins to see program results, an appreciation of the EAP function develops. Through training and ongoing consultation with the EAP practitioner, the program's benefits are realized and the supervisor's skills in dealing with the chemically dependent employee are sharpened.

Unless credibility is established with both employees and supervisors, the program's success will be limited. The EAP's objective is to return the employee to the workplace ready to do a day's work. This objective can be realized through strategic intervention—a function of the supervisor who has skillfully carried out those tasks essential to making an appropriate referral—and an EAP ready to provide assistance. Even the most resistant supervisors cannot argue with success. A high percentage of EAP referrals improve job performance and achieve lasting sobriety both on and off the job. The key to this success is simply using the job as a lever to get the employee to the EAP for assistance. As discussed in Chapter 5, the supervisor achieves this objective by applying those skills that are a function of being a supervisor: observation, documentation, and confrontation. Two more steps, referral (of the employee to the EAP) and reintegration (of the employee back to work) are added.

INVOLVING ALL THE KEY PLAYERS

Creating a climate that will encourage program utilization is a function of professional standards implementation, specifically good program design. This includes effective program management, union involvement, planned marketing strategies, and well-articulated policies and procedures congruent with existing personnel practices. In terms of effective program management and existing personnel practices, the supervisor must be able to communicate with the EAP in the same way that he or she communicates with any other work unit within the organization. The purpose of a staff function is to facilitate line management in getting the job done, and the EAP is a staff function. The supervisor should not have to learn medical, social-work, or counseling jargon, nor should a new set of policies be developed that "talk" a different language. The role and perception of the supervisor will influence the climate that ultimately determines program success. It is important, therefore, that program development include significant input from line supervisory personnel, and from union representatives if the organization is a union shop. It is management's responsibility to take this input and develop a program that reflects the objectives of the organization.

PROMOTION AND EDUCATION

The importance of a planned marketing strategy has been discussed in detail in Chapter 8. In marketing the EAP to reach those employees who might never be referred by supervisor, the organization is creating a climate that will encourage both self-referrals *and* supervisor-referrals. Educating the general employee population about drugs and alcohol serves to raise consciousness and brings the subject of chemical dependency out into the open. While the objective of promoting the EAP is to reach those employees who are experiencing problems, this is achieved through creating an environment where such employees are not stigmatized. The promotion strategy should be thought of as an ongoing campaign to remove the stigma associated with chemical dependency, and to create a climate of openness and awareness. The awareness allows individuals to make intelligent choices about the use of mood-altering chemicals, while openness respects the choices that others make. But most important, a well-orchestrated, organization-wide education program will reduce drinking and drug use in the workplace and encourage the use of the EAP when such problems do exist. The Federal Railroad Administration, for example, supported the launching of a nationwide program in 1985 designed to reduce the use and abuse of alcohol and drugs on the job. The program, which is called "Operation: Redblock," has been adopted by railroads throughout the country in an effort to change the railroad industry's image as a hard-drinking work culture and create an environment that frowns upon drug use. Up until that time, "Rule G," prohibited the use of or impairment from intoxicants on the job and "Rule E" placed the responsibility on coworkers to report Rule G violators to a company officer. An infraction of either rule is grounds for dismissal.

Operation: Redblock is geared toward prevention through education and peer pressure. Its success, however, can be attributed to the cooperative efforts of labor and management. Its prevention committees are sanctioned by unions and carriers, and while confrontation and referral of employees who violate Rule G are important committee functions, only 10 percent of the committee's time is spent on confrontation. The other 90 percent is spent organizing safety presentations and education programs.[2] While the adoption of EAPs by railroads is one of the objectives of the Operation: Redblock initiatives, the emphasis is on alcohol and drug education.

An ongoing promotion campaign should be designed to create an environment where the use of alcohol and/or drugs is not acceptable behavior and which provides information on where to turn for assistance if necessary. Print, posters, and bulletins are effective ways to reach the employee population. Articles should appear on a regular basis in the organization's newsletter, fliers can be enclosed with paychecks, and posters emphasizing "confidential help" should be strategically displayed. Many organizations make an effort to reach the employee's family by mailing announcements to the employee's home. Since the troubled employee is also a troubled family member, involving the family at this level can be important to early identification of the problem. This is especially important when the troubled employee is troubled not because of a personal chemical-dependency problem, but because a loved one at home is in trouble with alcohol or drugs. Reaching out to family members is a sure way to establish credibility with the employee population.

THE EAP AS A FUNCTION OF THE ENVIRONMENT

Program accessibility should be built into the program's design. Because the EAP provides a human service, the service should be available on any given day. Some organizations may not be large enough to justify a 24-hour program, but use an answering service during non-business hours. This is an inexpensive but very effective alternative. It is important, however, that calls from both troubled employees and supervisors be returned promptly, and appointments scheduled at the earliest possible convenience. Program credibility and program utilization are generated through prompt, professional service and visible results.

The EAP is most effective in a synchronous environment. Creating this environment is, to a great extent, the program's responsibility. Its procedures should be easy to understand and required paperwork should be kept at a minimum. Like any function or service of a work organization, the EAP must continuously evaluate its results and make appropriate changes in direction when necessary. The real value of an EAP is in its problem-solving ability. In order to continue to be of value, it must be ready to meet the needs of the employees as well as the needs of the managers and the supervisors expected to deal with the problems. The standards by which the EAP operates and the climate that it operates in will determine its effectiveness in reducing alcohol and drug-related job-performance problems. While the EAP alone will not solve the problem of chemical dependency in the workplace, it is an important part of the solution. It is a pragmatic approach to a human problem that is designed to provide a solution for both employee and employer. The chemically dependent person is provided an opportunity to receive assistance and both employee and employer profit as a result.

NOTES

1. John Dolan, "The Staffing Requirements of Employee Assistance Programs," in *Mental Wellness Programs for Employees*, eds. Richard H. Egdahl and Diana Chapman Walsh (New York: Springer-Verlag, 1980): 131.

2. Joan M. Rivard, "Operation: Redblock," *EAP Digest* (May/June 1990): 62. Based on *Operation: Redblock*, a monograph prepared by Stephen Eichler, Clifford M. Goldberg, Louise E. Kiew, and John P. Allen.

12

Unions, Management, and Joint Programs

LABOR UNIONS' DISTRUST OF MANAGEMENT EAPS

A management-operated employee assistance program is often viewed with suspicion by the bargaining unit. The unilateral formulation of a chemical-dependency policy and the implementation of an EAP might even be in violation of the collective bargaining agreement. Any action taken by the employer, in fact, that has not been negotiated at the bargaining table could be considered a violation of the terms and conditions of employment as defined by contract. Referring a union employee to the company EAP for an evaluation, for example, might be grounds to file a grievance. At the very least, the union member is certain to talk to his union representative before going.

Union members are not likely to seek help voluntarily from a management-operated program for problems related to alcohol and/or drug use or abuse. This is especially true if the employee is in a safety-sensitive position where the use of mood-altering chemicals could result in termination. Union representatives will seldom, if ever, refer a union member to a management EAP. The exception to this is where the EAP has earned the trust of the union over a long period of time and the program's credibility has been established.

While joint union-management programs have proven successful in both helping the chemically dependent employee and eliminating time-consuming, no-win grievance procedures, EAPs without union input do not enjoy the same level of cooperation. The EAP is frequently seen as a device of the personnel department for the purpose of reducing costs and/or facilitating compliance with progressive disciplinary action procedures. This is true even when the program is a function of the organization's medical department. Consequently, the management EAP is likely to be used by unions only as a last resort to circumvent disciplinary action against union members. This is not to say that all management programs are eschewed by union members, but establishing any level of trust may take years to achieve.

The union is, of course, right in part. While a professionally sanctioned EAP is not likely to allow itself to be used against any employee, most EAPs are a function of management with an objective to reduce the costs of alcohol and drug related problems in the workplace. The union can appreciate management's objective, yet it views the problem from a different perspective. It sees the chemically dependent employee as a brother or sister in trouble or as a human problem that requires intervention rather than as a cost problem that must be contained. Union representatives talk of helping those suffering from alcoholism and drug abuse while management executives talk of reducing the cost of chemical dependency in the workplace. One such union officer says:

I believe that this most dreaded disease, alcoholism, can be overcome with the helpful compassion and understanding of our fellow brother and sister human beings.[1]

From a management point of view, however, the focus is cost containment. A staff person from a major service company says:

I can't even estimate what drug use has cost this company. I think it's the biggest problem in industry today. Nothing else is even in second place compared to it.[2]

The union executive speaks of "compassion and understanding" and the corporate executive talks of company "cost." While joint union-management programs transcend these differences in the interest of common sense, a unilateral program, whether it be a union member assistance program (MAP) or a management program, seldom gets the opportunity to communicate with the other side. Once a management-sponsored EAP is established, it is not likely to be later developed into a true labor-management program. Unless the union is invited to participate in the development of policies, procedures, and program implementation at the onset, the EAP will be viewed as a management program with all of its limitations. These limitations can be reduced, however, by inviting union participation at any point in time. This participation can be formal or informal. An EAP advisory committee of union and management representatives has worked well in many organizations. Even when management is absorbing the entire cost of the operation it is advisable to form such a committee. A cooperative effort will improve the EAP's potential effectiveness and prove more cost effective in the long run.

JOINT UNION-MANAGEMENT EAPS ARE BETTER

Approximately 16.5 percent of the American labor force is represented by bargaining agents.[3] The labor unions serving as bargaining agents for these employees negotiate with employers on wages, working conditions, and whatever else may be in the best interest of both union and worker. Sometimes, however, these interests are in conflict with the health and welfare of the employee represented. An employee who is suspected of drinking on the job, for example, is likely to get full union support in fighting such a rule violation. If the disciplinary action for such a charge is termination, this support is seldom, if ever, compromised.

Everyone loses in these cases. Management frequently loses its case against the employee, the union must defend an employee it knows it will be called upon to defend again, and the employee loses an opportunity to take care of a serious problem. The progression of the problem is certain, deterioration of job performance is inevitable, costly grievance proceedings continue, and in the long run, the employee loses the job anyway.

In joint union-management programs this will not happen. The troubled employee gets a clear message from both sides that unacceptable job performance is not tolerated by management and that self-destructive behavior is not tolerated by the union. Many union-management EAPs exist in the United States and such programs are bound by a joint policy signed by both the chief executive officer and the union president. This cooperative effort is made clear to the union members through literature, meetings, and by distributing copies of the signed policy statement including procedures governing the agreement. Many union programs also distribute brochures to shop stewards and delegates that emphasize the importance of a cooperative program. One such brochure conveys the following message:

Alcoholic workers often cause accidents and increase production costs through poor workmanship and absenteeism, giving industry its so-called "multi-billion dollar hangover." In addition to avoiding this "hangover," both union and company also like to avoid getting bogged down in a maze of time-consuming grievances related to alcoholism which could be prevented with a formal cooperative program. Finally, neither party relishes the arbitration costs associated with these grievances, money which could be better devoted to strengthen an active rehabilitation program.[4]

Joint programs have been shown to be more effective than union-only or management-only programs for several reasons. First, the program obtains greater visibility. This is likely to result in greater acceptance by union, non-union, and supervisory personnel. Another reason cited is that joint programs are less likely to be accused of discriminatory practices, selectively giving employees a second chance. While this should not happen in any organization with any type of program, it remains, nevertheless, a consideration. A third reason why joint programs increase their potential effectiveness is that a greater appreciation of the chemical-dependency problem and its consequences for industry, business, and the work organization is realized. The dissemination of information to all concerned and the education process is better facilitated through a cooperative program effort. Finally, the combined efforts of management and labor, by presenting a unified posture with respect to the afflicted individual, maximizes the probability of a successful outcome.[5]

CHEMICAL DEPENDENCY IS A UNION PROBLEM

Employee chemical dependence is as much of a problem for the union as it is for the employer. In one assembly plant surveyed, more than 48.6 percent of the grievances filed were alcohol or drug related.[6] In an effort to reduce both the grievances and the alcoholism/drug problems in the workplace, the union teamed up with management and formed joint labor-management programs at plants where the union had employees. Many such joint EAPs now exist in the United States and the contractual language emphasizes the human aspect of these programs:

The Company and Union jointly recognize alcoholism [chemical dependence] as an illness which can be successfully treated. It is also recognized that it is for the best interest of the employee, the Company and the Union that this illness be treated and controlled under the existing bargaining contractual agreement....A Labor-Management Program will be established for the purpose of helping the individual with this disease to recover. The program is to be designed for rehabilitation and not elimination of the employee. Any program administrators (by whatever title) will be selected with equal representation from Management and from the Union, and will be allowed sufficient time with pay to perform their program duties.[7]

The traditional role of the union representative is to represent the interests of the employee. This includes protecting the wages, hours, and benefits of its members, and insuring acceptable working conditions. But many unions also realize that alcoholic and the drug-abusing employees have been able to play their union representatives and the company supervisors off against each other so that they may continue their drinking and/or drug use without interruption. Therefore, it is essential for both union representatives and the supervisors to understand the nature of alcoholism and drug abuse. The supervisor and the union representative together "hold the key to the greatest motivating tool yet found" to get the chemically dependent person to realize that he or she has a problem and to seek help.[8] This "tool" is, of course, the employee's desire to keep his or her job.

JOINT EAPs: COOPERATION VERSUS CONFRONTATION

If an employee charged with an an alcohol- or drug-related rule violation denies the problem, then the union is placed in the awkward position of having to support the employee's denial. Everyone may know that the employee's drinking or drug abuse is the real problem, but there is no neutral ground on which union and management can confront the issue. The joint EAP provides such a forum and, in most cases, eliminates such problems. Frequently at the urging of the union delegate, the chemical-dependent employee gets help before job performance deteriorates to the point where disciplinary action is imminent.

In setting their differences aside and dealing with chemical dependency as a problem for all concerned, both union and management stand to win. Not only do both sides benefit in terms of both cost reduction and employee welfare, but coming together on these kinds of issues opens the door to discussing other problems that might otherwise call for hard negotiating. Experience has shown that the best climate in which to negotiate anything is one of cooperation rather than confrontation.[9] While having a joint labor-management employee assistance program will not end the ritual of hammering out key labor accords in marathon, round-the-clock bargaining sessions, it will demonstrate that some issues can be resolved in a cooperative fashion. In this way joint union-management programs provide a benefit to both the work organization and the labor union beyond the human and financial importance of such programs.

NOTES

1. International Association of Machinists and Aerospace Workers, "Occupational Alcoholism Programs Thru Union Contracts" (Offset).

2. John Brecher and Erik Ipsen, "Taking Drugs on the Job," *Newsweek* (August 22, 1983): 52.

3. Bureau of Labor Statistics, estimated 1991, *The World Almanac* 1990, 108.

4. Alcoholism: Programs with Promise (Pittsburgh, PA: United Steel Workers of America): 18.

5. Madeleine L. Tramm, "Union-Based Programs," in *The Human Resources Management Handbook/Principles and Practice of Employee Assistance Programs,* ed. Samuel H. Klarreich, James L. Francek, and C. Eugene Moore (New York: Praeger, 1985): 97.

6. Alcoholism Council of Greater New York Fact Sheet.

7. "Occupational," International.

8. Ibid., 16, 17.

9. William S. Duncan, *The EAP Manual* (New York: National Council on Alcoholism, 1982): 11.

13

Testing for Drugs:
A Nebulous Solution

DRUG TESTING ENCOURAGED BY THE GOVERNMENT

Workplace drug use was at an all-time high in the mid-1980s and so was the consensus that drug testing would be the solution to this growing problem. Encouraged by the President's Commission on Organized Crime, government agencies were urged to test employees while private sector work organizations, spirited by the government's endorsement, scrambled in search of toxicology screening laboratories that would take on the job. The commission's message was plain and simple: Those employees who failed the test would be disciplined.[1]

The solution seemed so simple it was a wonder that no one thought of it sooner. Establish a drug-testing policy, communicate the policy to the employee population, develop procedures, and begin testing. Urine testing, as opposed to the more invasive blood testing, would be the method of analysis. Employees who were using controlled substances would stop using and those who could not stop would either be referred to treatment or disciplined. Drug testing would be a simple, neat, and expedient route to ending a costly workplace problem.

The drug testing solution can be summed up in a quotation from H. L. Mencken: "For every problem there is one solution which is simple, neat, and wrong."[2] While drug testing may play a role in addressing the problem, it is not now, and will never become, the solution. It is riddled with complications ranging from cost considerations to legal issues to program implementation. If we consider that the threat of police action, family disgrace, fiscal insolvency, health problems, and even death are insufficient to deter rational, intelligent people from using drugs, how can we expect that a workplace drug testing policy will? The National Football League's drug testing policy provides a visible and valuable lesson: Testing does not eliminate drug use.[3]

MOST ORGANIZATIONS DON'T TEST FOR DRUGS

It appears that both government and private sector employers have learned this lesson. Many through their own limited success with costly, unwieldy drug testing programs. On November 18, 1988, in response to the continuing spread of drug abuse, President Reagan signed into law the Anti-Drug Abuse Act of 1988 (Title V, Subtitle D of P.L. 100–690).[4] This act, in its final form, addresses such issues as illegal money laundering, anti-child pornography, obscenity, and drug-free workplace requirements for federal contractors. The Drug-Free Workplace Act of 1988 (DFWA), a provision of The Anti-Drug Abuse Act of 1988, went into effect on March 18, 1989. (See Chapter 4 for more on the Drug-Free Workplace Act.) While this important piece of legislation became law only three years after the President's Commission on Organized Crime recommended drug testing, drug testing is not included in its provisions! Both the Congress and the Executive Branch were judicious enough to exclude drug testing as a requirement for compliance. With three years to reflect on the pros and cons of drug testing, the Drug-Free Workplace Act became law without it.

Drug testing is used, nevertheless, in both government and private sector work organizations. As discussed in Chapter 4, both the Department of Transportation (DOT) and the Department of Defense (DOD) test employees for controlled substances.

The DOT, under the Department of Health and Human Services' "Mandatory Guidelines for Federal Workplace Drug Testing Programs," issued regulations requiring anti-drug programs in the aviation motor carrier, railroad, maritime, mass transit, and pipeline industries to conduct drug testing (Federal Register, Department of Transportation Requirements, November 21, 1988). The requirement for all of its agencies to establish drug-testing programs can be linked directly to a well-publicized crash in 1987 of two trains in Chase, Maryland, in which the engineer at fault tested positive for marijuana.[5] The department's operating administrations (Federal Aviation Administration, Federal Highway Administration, Federal Railroad Administration, United States Coast Guard, Urban Mass Transportation Administration, and Research and Special Programs Administration) are covered under this rule (49 CFR Part 40, et al).[6]

The DOD, under 48 CFR Parts 223 and 252, requires that:

The Contractor shall establish a program that provides for testing for the use of illegal drugs by employees in safety sensitive positions. The extent of and criteria for such testing shall be determined by the Contractor based on considerations that include the Nature of the work performed under the contract, the employee's duties, the efficient use of Contractor resources, and the risks to public health, safety, national security that could result from the failure of an employee adequately to discharge his or her position.

A relatively small number of private-sector work organizations have drug testing programs. The larger the organization, the greater the chance it will have a program. In a survey that sorted companies by total number of employees, only 0.8 percent with fewer than ten employees tested for drugs compared to 50.8 percent of those with more than one thousand employees. Although 50.8 percent appears high, the one-thousand-plus group represents only 5,600 companies, while the fewer-than-ten-employee group represents more than 3,140,900 companies—69 percent of the 4,542,800 companies in the United States. The survey shows that 3.2 percent of all companies test for drugs.[7]

If we were to exclude the fewer-than-ten group from the survey, the total percentage of companies that do drug testing would change from 3.2 percent to 8.6 percent. Even so, this means that more than 91.4 percent of all companies in the United States do not test for drugs. The 3.2 percent of the companies that test for drugs represent 19.6 percent of the workforce. From this perspective, 80.4 percent of all employees in the United States do not work for companies that test for drug use. It should be noted, however, that recent random testing mandates implemented by both the Department of Defense and the Department of Transportation might encourage large private sector companies to consider testing.

LABOR UNIONS CHALLENGE DRUG TESTING

Labor unions unilaterally oppose drug testing. A work organization that announces plans to test its employees will get opposition from the bargaining agent. Even when the employer's plan meets all legal requirements, conducts tests only "for cause," and implements a non-punitive program for individuals who test positive, such a plan is certain to get the attention of the bargaining unit.

The following is a statement by the American Federation of Labor and Congress of Industrial Organizations:

No one doubts that workers who suffer from drug addiction—or alcoholism—need, and benefit from, well-conceived and soundly administered treatment programs. Likewise, no one doubts that workers impaired by either of these illnesses can pose health and safety hazards on the job. But it is equally clear that drug testing is subject to numerous objections. Particularly if the tests are on a random basis, the process cuts deeply into individual privacy rights. There are serious questions about testing accuracy; and a false positive report can stigmatize its victim for life. Contrary to the general belief, drug testing cannot establish whether a worker is currently addicted to a drug, is under the influence of a drug, or is unable to do his/her work because of drug use. Testing that leads to discipline rather than treatment gives the employer broad power to punish the employees who are doing their job because the employer disapproves of their off-duty conduct.[8]

The American Civil Liberties Union also opposes drug testing. Their position as quoted from an ACLU briefing paper is as follows:

The American Civil Liberties Union opposes indiscriminate urine testing because the process is both unfair and unnecessary. It is unfair to force millions of American workers who are not even suspected of using drugs, and whose job performance is satisfactory, "to prove their innocence" through a degrading and uncertain procedure that violates personal privacy. It is unnecessary because such tests, since they cannot detect current impairment, add nothing to an employer's ability to evaluate or predict job performance.[9]

The ACLU cites the Fourth Amendment to the Constitution of the United States as the foundation of their argument against drug testing. It says that it may be the "easiest way to identify drug users, but it is also by far the most un-American." It goes on to say that urine testing does not prevent drug use and in some cases may even be counterproductive in forcing drug abusers to avoid detection rather than seek help. The ACLU believes that education and voluntary rehabilitation are tried and true methods that prevent drug use and help those addicts in need.[10]

The Fourth Amendment, which protects the rights of individuals against illegal search and seizure, has also been cited by the Legal Action Center in their position on drug testing. In a policy statement on drug testing, the LAC states:

Many employers have instituted mandatory urine testing programs as a way to eliminate drug abuse in the workplace. However, mandatory urine testing programs are not by themselves an appropriate or responsible way to screen applicants or employees for substance abuse. Mandatory urine testing programs are fraught with problems. There are questions about how accurate testing is, what a positive result means, and whether mandatory urine testing is legal.[11]

Advocates for drug testing are likely to take the position that such measures are in the interest of public safety. In 1985, three percent of the Fortune 500 companies tested for drugs. By 1988, 50 percent were performing some type of drug test on prospective or current employees.[12] In 1991, drug testing remains at about 50 percent.

The increase in drug testing followed several accidents, the prevailing mood of society, and President Reagan's call for the testing of federal employees in an effort to secure a drug-free federal workplace. In addition to the two-train accident in Chase, Maryland, that prompted mandatory drug testing in the Department of Transportation, private corporations responded to on-the-job fatalities that may have been prevented had the employee been drug free. One such case involved a production line leader at Philips Industries called to fix a jammed metal press. Against all safety regulations, she leaned into the press and began banging on the release. The release unjammed before she was able to get out from under the press, crushing and killing her instantly. An autopsy confirmed what company officials had feared: she had high levels of cocaine in her blood.[13]

Southern Pacific Railroad, in response to several accidents at other railroads, established a drug testing program. The railroad's criteria for testing was "reasonable suspicion" of drug use. It also attempted random testing for a period of time but found the practice too disruptive to work routines. Although the random testing program was quickly dropped, it resulted in a lawsuit filed by a computer operator who was fired after she refused to sign an agreement to be tested. The company lost the case.[14]

DRUG TESTING VERSUS EMPLOYEE ASSISTANCE PROGRAMS

Approximately 17 million employees work for organizations that test for drugs while 26 million are employed by companies covered by employee assistance programs. Almost 12 million work for companies that have both employee assistance and drug-testing programs. This leaves almost 54 million employees who work for organizations without drug testing or employee assistance program.[15] It appears that most organizations testing their employees also provide employee assistance services. This is important to the success of a drug-testing program. A work organization that does testing but does not provide an opportunity for help will defeat its purpose. Such programs are punitive in nature and serve only to identify and discipline employees who might otherwise respond to assistance. A drug-testing program with no provision for treatment will not just affect those employees and family members in need of help, it will alienate all employees. Not because all employees are sympathetic to the treatment needs of the chemically dependent employee, but because such a policy is symptomatic of a deeper indifference to all employee needs. This organizational insensitivity is certain to show up in various ways throughout the company.

Some observers report that testing can also create an easy out for coworkers and supervisors who can now rationalize that the system will take care of the problem, absolving them of responsibility. Drug testing can also deter employees from seeking help. The "us against them" situation it creates and the emphasis on the punitive aspects of the problem can discourage employees from coming forward to seek help.[16]

The New York State system has adapted a three-pronged approach to developing a drug-free workplace program: (1) Drug testing and deterrence, (2) Rehabilitation, including health benefit design considerations and New York's employee assistance program, and (3) Education.

The state has rejected a massive testing program in favor of testing only current employees in selected occupations. Very limited applicant testing is now in use and that policy is under review. It views drug testing as just one tool that must be used with care and with regard for the constitutional protections of personal privacy and the rights of union involvement, confidentiality, and procedural integrity.[17]

The Employee Assistance Professionals Association, Inc., has developed a procedural approach for addressing alcohol and drug abuse in the workplace. This approach was designed specifically for those work organizations that plan to use drug testing as a tool. The approach, in diagram form, takes the reader through the planning and implementation phases, beginning with an organizational assessment of the problem and moving on through the forming of a labor-management committee, policy development, insurance review, EAP design, resource development, drug testing program design, training and program monitoring. The model, first developed in 1987, cites "reasonable suspicion" as the only criterion for testing. The EAPA continues to maintain this position in the 1990s although it acknowledges that the new federal rules on testing in the Department of Transportation and Department of Defense may have been developed in the interest of public safety.

While most work organizations that test employees do pre-employment and reasonable-cause testing, there are several options available to the employer. These include:

1. Test the entire employee population at regularly scheduled intervals
2. Conduct random testing
3. Test as part of a physical examination
4. Test for cause or reasonable suspicion (inappropriate behavior, poor job performance, etc.)
5. Test after an accident
6. Test employees holding safety-sensitive positions
7. Pre-employment testing

If we consider each of these criteria and how it impacts on all parties concerned, it becomes clear why some are acceptable and others are not. Testing all employees, for example, is simply not cost effective. Even using a less expensive method (discussed below) to "screen" an entire organization can add up when you consider both laboratory cost and staff time. Positive findings will have to be tested again using more costly testing techniques. Nevertheless, several large corporations have elected to test their entire employee population. Motorola is testing its 60,000 U.S.-based employees over a three-year period. Texas Instruments began universal testing of its 52,000 employees in 1990.[18] As part of a routine physical examination, many other work organizations have successfully integrated drug testing.

Reasonable and objective standards related to job performance or fitness for duty—the reasonable suspicion standard—are favored by the courts before testing is permitted (New Jersey v. T.L.O., 469 U.S. 325 (1985); Matter of Patchogue-Medford Congress of Teachers v. Board of Education, Supra). On-the-job accidents fall into this category.

In 1989, the United States Supreme Court looked further at the issue of safety sensitive positions in which the expectation of privacy was diminished. Late in 1989, the Appellate Division of New York State upheld random drug testing of all New York City correction officers as constitutional, based on the sensitive security of the job (Sellig et al. v. Kohler et al.).

If an employer determines that drug testing is appropriate for job applicants or current employees, great attention must be paid to the procedures under which the testing is conducted. The integrity of the testing procedures is vital to the validity of the testing program. Among the issues that need to be addressed are:

Integrity of the test samples
Chain of custody of the samples
Confidentiality of test results
Number of samples required
Qualifications of the testing service
Follow-up testing after a positive finding
Recipient(s) of test results
Actions triggered by positive results [19]

ACCURACY, RELIABILITY, AND LIMITATIONS

All drug testing falls into one of three broad testing methods: Chromatography, Antibody or Immunoassay, and Gas Chromatography-Mass Spectrometry. Most experts agree that the Gas Chromatography-Mass Spectrometry (GC-MS) method of testing is both accurate and reliable. This method is expensive, however, and is used primarily as a confirmation test. The oldest and most widely used of the chromatographic tests is called Thin Layer Chromatography (TLC). This method, as well as the antibody or immunoassay testing methods, are generally used for "screening."[20] It is important to note that whatever testing methodology is used, a positive result of a urine test does not confirm impairment while on duty (see Table 13.1). The National Institute on Drug Abuse (NIDA) recognizes that "The positive results of a urine screen cannot be used to prove intoxication or impaired performance."

Table 13.1
Drug Detection Times

Drug Type	Daily Dose	Half Life	Detectable Amount	Detection Time Limits
Amphetamines	100 mg	4 Hrs	100 ng	To 3 Days
Cannabis	50 mg	24 Hrs	50 ng	To 7 Days
Cocaine	500 mg	4 Hrs	100 ng	To 3 Days
Narcotics	100 mg	4 Hrs	100 ng	To 3 Days
PCP	50 mg	48 Hrs	50 ng	To 14 Days
Sedatives	100 mg	24 Hrs	100 ng	To 10 Days

Source: An AFL-CIO Guide: "Drug Testing on the Job."

The accuracy and reliability of a drug test depends upon several factors: integrity of the sample, testing methodology, technician's qualifications and skill, and chain of custody. If there is a breakdown in any of these areas, the test becomes invalid. A technically sensible and cost-efficient approach to drug analysis requires the availability and utilization of both immunologic techniques and chromatographic methodologies in a complementary manner. Such an approach insures the avoidance of false positives yet is cost effective because GC-MS, the most expensive method, is used only for those samples that are positive and require confirmation.[21] Screening for a panel of drugs costs $10 to $15. The confirmation test cost about $35 per drug.[22]

Employers are expected to do everything in their power to ensure a safe working environment. This includes compliance with all the federal, state, and local laws that govern such matters. One such law is the federal Drug-Free Workplace Act of 1988. While this law applies only to those employers that are receiving grants or funds directly from the federal government, many employers are following the guidelines in this act to develop a drug-free work environment. And while drug testing is not a provision of this act, many organizations have incorporated drug testing programs in their effort to create an environment free of drugs.

The presence of drug-impaired employees threatens the safety of both the impaired employees and their coworkers. It is a costly problem that directly affects the success of the organization. Employee assistance, including education and rehabilitation, are proven strategies in addressing this problem. The challenge of developing and maintaining a drug-free workplace will depend to a great extent on the organization's commitment to such efforts. There are no shortcuts. If drug testing is added to these efforts, it should be restricted to a narrow range of situations. Overly ambitious and haphazardly administered drug-testing programs will undermine both the integrity of the program and the work organization it represents.

NOTES

1. Walter Scanlon, "Crime Commission Solution Inadequate," *The AL-MACAN* 16, No. 10 (October 1986): 17–18.

2. Nancy L. Hodes, "Drugs in the Workplace: New York State Is Meeting the Challenge," *Employee Benefits Journal*, March 1990, 21–32.

3. Ibid.

4. Legal Action Center, "The Drug-Free Workplace Act," Background Materials (New York: Legal Action Center, 1989).

5. "FAA Releases Airline Drug Testing Regs," *The ALMACAN*, 19, No. 3 (March 1989): 15.

6. Portfolio of Information on the 1988 Drug-Free Workplace Act and Federal EAP Regulations (Employee Assistance Program Association, 1989), 16–18.

7. Bureau of Labor Statistics, "Drug Testing and Employee Assistance Programs," *World Almanac and Book of Facts*, (New York: Pharos Books, 1990), 105.

8. American Federation of Labor and Congress of Industrial Organizations, *Drug and Alcohol Testing on the Job* (Washington, DC: President Lane Kirkland's office), 2.

9. *ACLU Briefing Paper: Drug Testing in the Workplace* (New York: American Civil Liberties Union, 1987).

10. Ibid.

11. *The Legal Action Center's Statement on Drug Testing* (New York: Legal Action Center, 1990).

12. "Drug Testing: Safety Boon Or Moral Bust," *Health Action Managers*, January 18, 1988, 1.

13. Ibid., 6.

14. Ibid., 7.

15. Bureau, "Drug," *World*, 105.

16. Hordes, "Drugs," *Journal*.

17. Ibid.

18. *U.S.A. Today*, "Drug Testing" May 22, 1990, 3A.

19. Hordes, "Drugs," *Journal*.

20. American Federation, Drug & Alcohol, Washington, 6.

21. Kenneth R. Sandler, M.D., "The Role of the Clinical Laboratory in Diagnosing and Treating Substance Abuse," *Biopsychiatric Insights on Substance Abuse*, (Princeton, NJ: Psychiatric Diagnostic Laboratories of America, Inc., No Date), 68–75.

22. Interview with Stephan Haupt, Eastern Laboratories Ltd., Port Washington, NY, July 1990.

14

The Corporate Culture

KNOW THE ORGANIZATION BEFORE IMPLEMENTING A PROGRAM

The EAP, like any other department within the organization, must position itself within the existing corporate culture. It must fit into the existing system of shared values and organizational beliefs that interact with a company's people, organizational structures, and control systems to produce behavioral norms. Simply stated, it must fit in with what is important, with how things work and, finally, the way things are done.[1]

In a company where the employee population is organized and represented by a bargaining agent, a joint labor-management EAP will be more effective than a management-operated program. In addition to those reasons for involving the union as discussed in Chapter 12, excluding the union from participation is ignoring the influence of the union on the corporate culture. The corporate culture of any organization, union or non-union, will ultimately determine whether or not the EAP will fit in. If the concept is not accepted by those individuals within the organization who wield the stamp of approval, then the program's effectiveness will be limited. The EAP may continue to exist and even reach a small percentage of troubled employees, but those referrals are likely to be employees in the latter stages of chemical dependency. The program will be used as a dumping ground rather than a management tool that helps supervisors do their job more effectively.

An EAP is going to be less effective in a company that does not have a strong corporate culture. Shared values, and organizational beliefs provide an environment that is conducive to good human resource management and that is consistent with EAP goals and objectives. The EAP concept is not easy to understand in that it takes what might seem a simple solution—firing the nonproductive employee—and trades it for a somewhat complicated process—treating the nonproductive employee. It places a condition on the existing progressive disciplinary procedures adding a step that might be considered an inconvenience by some and ignored by others. Unless the corporate culture views the EAP as an important function of the organization that is not so different from other operations within the organization, the concept is likely to fail.

Poorer-performing companies with dysfunctional or no identifiable corporate culture will beget poor performing or marginal EAPs. While an organization with a strong corporate culture will either accept or reject an idea, a weak culture will neither accept nor reject it. It will use the EAP at whim and for whatever reason prevails, usually having little to do with cost containment or with human values. Unlike those "excellent companies" described in *In Search of Excellence*, these companies usually focus on internal politics and numbers rather than on products and people. On the operations level this translates into taking action to meet a personal need rather than to meet an organizational objective. As one corporate executive put it, "You know, the problem [in a poor-performing company] is *every* decision is being made for the first time."[2]

While the concept of employee assistance programming may be sound in theory, the existing corporate culture may render it ineffective. Unless the policies and procedures on chemical dependency become an integral part of all the existing human resource management policies and procedures, every decision to use the EAP will be "made for the first time." The decision will be individual rather than organizational.

THE MANAGEMENT FACTOR

The employee assistance program serves to facilitate and make effective the company's policy on dealing with alcohol- and drug-related job-performance problems. The organization's motives for having an EAP may be to help troubled employees, to save corporate dollars or a combination of the two. The idea for a program may come out of the human resources department, the medical department or the labor relations department. Whatever the organization's motives are for considering an EAP, one fact is crucial to an effective program:

Management support is essential and without it, the EAP is simply corporate window dressing.

It would seem that an existing EAP would have to have the support of management for it to exist in the first place and if did not, it would simply be eliminated. This is not always true. An existing EAP may be the vestige of the last "regime," and the existing policy statement on chemical-dependency issued by the previous CEO may have yellowed with time. Any reference made to it may, indeed, be out-of-sync with existing norms and provoke negative reactions. Or the EAP may be in a state, federal, or municipal agency where the provision of such services are required by law. Just because the program is required does not necessarily mean that management wants it. Or it may be in an organization where the management structure is bureaucratic and changing anything is virtually impossible. Finally, the EAP may limp along in a democratic-style organizational structure where the management does not support the idea but cannot do much about it.

The point here is that marginal EAPs do continue to exist for an assortment of reasons having little to do with economic *or* humanistic objectives. The greatest resistance to an EAP, however, is probably that it is perceived as different from other organizational functions. This difference is primarily in management's perceptions which are based on image and language associated with health-care agencies. Health care agencies, and by extension EAPs, use words like "help," "sick," "disabled," "diagnosis," "treatment" and "aftercare." By contrast, work organizations "get the job done" with "efficiency," embodying "hard work," "tough decisions," and "profit."[3] The EAP is not perceived as a business management function but rather as a health care function, operating on a not-for-profit tract with objectives that hardly resemble those formulated in the board room. This perception, unfortunately, is often reinforced by EAP staff members. Practitioners eager to communicate the human value of reaching troubled employees sometimes overuse clinical terminology that alienates both management and supervisory staff members. Most EAP professionals do not make this mistake and are, in fact, quite skillful at wearing two hats, changing from clinical to managerial roles on cue. The training and experience that makes this transition possible is a prerequisite to working in the field of employee assistance. Work organizations are now encouraged to hire practitioners who can demonstrate EAP competencies. An examination administered by the Professional Testing Corporation in New York City qualifies candidates upon passing with a Certified Employee Assistance Professional (CEAP) credential.

Since the EAP exists as a work unit within the general organization, it might appear that the EAP will reflect a similar management perspective. Management which adopts organizational goals such as profit, production, and cost control, however, can conflict with an EAP staff that identifies goals such as stress resolution and behavior modification. If it is perceived that EAP objectives diverge from organizational objectives, then management staff will not support or cooperate with the program. This may show through a lack of financial support of EAP staff and programs, poor cooperation in personnel decisions, limited referrals from management and supervisory personnel, and a general disregard for confidentiality.[4] This perception, however, is likely to be based on preconceived notions rather than on existing EAP practices. The EAP actually has two goals—one is functional and the other is organizational. The functional goal is successful treatment and recovery while the organizational goal is improved job performance and productivity. These goals are usually achieved simultaneously once the employee is referred to the EAP, but getting the employee there is part of the treatment process and this is where the resistance often begins.

Supervisory resistance to EAP utilization is an inevitable outgrowth of management indifference. Without management support of policy and program, the EAP will be underutilized and supervisors will continue to deal with job-performance problems in whatever way they have in the past. In most cases this means that early identification of the troubled employee will not be practiced and only those late-stage chemically dependent persons will be referred. Without management support the EAP is not likely to have an aggressive supervisory training program, and without training the supervisor will not know how to address the problem.

Management indifference to policy and program leads to a corporate culture that responds to the EAP concept with: "That's not the way we do things around here." This is particularly frustrating to a supervisor who knows better and attempts to deal with a troubled employee in the "right" way, by noting the employee's deteriorating job performance, conducting an intervention interview, and making an appropriate referral to the company EAP. Unless the action is supported by *current* policy and has a firm and current management endorsement, the supervisor—especially a first-line supervisor—might be considered by colleagues and subordinates to be overzealous and out-of-step with accepted supervisory practices. In some work environments the supervisor may, indeed, be viewed as a "stool pigeon" or "rat" for making such a referral.

THE BEST EAPs ARE PLANNED EAPs

Some EAP advocates might defend the existence of a program in an unfriendly corporate environment with the rationale that any EAP is better than no EAP at all. On the contrary, a program that is not effective may be worse than having no program at all. A poorly administered EAP, for whatever reasons, is harmful both for the organization and for the troubled employee. Supervisory training will be nonexistent or ineffectual, research/evaluation is unlikely and case management may be selective and inconsistent. Legal issues and ethical standards may be ignored, insurance plans may not provide adequate treatment coverage, and the program may actually "enable" continued drug and/or alcohol abuse rather than contain it. Most importantly, it may keep a troubled employee from getting the help he or she needs.

Installing an EAP is a major decision that cannot be taken lightly. Legal details, treatment issues, confidentiality requirements, training programs, insurance coverage, personnel policies, marketing plans, outreach strategies, and program scope are some of the details, to mention a few, that must be addressed before the first troubled employee comes through the door. In addition, program policies, procedures, training, treatment, standards of performance, productivity controls, and communications must come together in an orchestrated fashion to form an effective company-wide approach to alcohol- and drug-related problems in the workplace. Regardless of the size and scope of the program, the EAP is a serious undertaking and a full commitment by management is essential to its success. While the program must also fit into the corporate culture of the organization, corporate culture is influenced by corporate management. Even in an organization where the culture is old and the management is new, the success of the EAP will depend on whether or not the leadership says, "This is the way things are done around here."

All organizations should provide services that will help troubled employees and, at the same time, reduce the cost of alcohol- and drug-related problems in the workplace. This is an old idea yet it fits into a new human resource management method called "corporate due process." While this method focuses on the resolution of employee grievances that might otherwise result in costly arbitration, its goal is to ensure equity and justice on the job.[5] The EAP also provides equity and justice on the job in affording the troubled employee the opportunity to get treatment. Employee assistance programming and corporate due process have at least two features in common: Both provide help for employees and reduce costs for the organization.

Whether the EAP is contracted or internal, the concept makes sense from both an economic and humanistic point of view. But to apply the concept effectively the organization should first examine its needs and shape the program to those needs. To drop a program into an organization without first conducting an audit would be like placing a product in the marketplace without first researching the market's needs. The organization is the marketplace and the EAP is the product or service to be offered. It stands to reason, then, that factors such as employee composition, union presence, management commitment, organization size, legal constraints, and community resources be examined as the first step in planning a program. Most importantly, will the existing corporate culture accept or reject the concept? In light of this concern, what can be done to ensure the EAPs success? In preparing and being aware of those hurdles that might otherwise render a program ineffective, the EAP improves its potential to achieve its objective.

NOTES

1. Bro Uttal, "The Corporate Culture Vultures," *Fortune* (October 17, 1983), 66.

2. Thomas J. Peters and Robert H. Waterman Jr., *In Search of Excellence* (New York: Harper & Row, 1982), 76.

3. Paul M. Roman, "Barriers to the Initiation of Employee Alcoholism Programs," in *NIAAA Research Monograph 8/Occupational Alcoholism: A Review of Research Issues* (Washington, DC: Government Printing Office, 1982), 149.

4. Googins and Kurtz, 1981, cited by Paul Steel, "Assessing Employee Assistance Programs: Intra- and Extra-Organizational Influences," in *EAP Research: An Annual of Research and Research Issues*, 1, C, ed. Howard Grimes (Troy, MI: Performance Resource Press, 1984): 37, 38.

5. David W. Ewing, "Justice on the Job" (Boston: Harvard Business School Press, 1989).

15

EAPs Make
Corporate Sense

EAPs HELP PEOPLE

The benefits and value of having an EAP can be expressed in both economic and humanistic terms. A financial analyst will evaluate the program's effectiveness in terms of cost reduction while the medical director might review the quality of care provided. One discipline would measure success in dollars while the other would see the health and safety benefits. An economic model would present the EAP's net present value while the humanistic model would argue for good health.

Both the economic model and the humanistic model are valid measures of an EAP's performance and effectiveness. It is difficult, in fact, to separate the two in that many of the human benefits are impossible to quantify yet undoubtedly increase productivity. Improved morale, for example, cannot be put into a calculator and goodwill has no tangible dollar value. (Actually, management accountants do have a formula for determining the goodwill value of an organization.) While cost containment is undeniably a major factor in installing and maintaining an EAP, the human factor is often the major impetus behind employee assistance programming. Recovery rates rather than dollars saved are often used to demonstrate a program's success. A manual by the National Council on Alcoholism reported in 1982 that managements often install such programs for "altruistic reasons," and that "the principal business of these programs is saving lives and by extension, families"; that an effective employee assistance program motivates the employee to "accept the treatment which holds the only hope of survival."[1] In the 1990s, this still holds true.

While there is a cost-benefit side to helping troubled employees, the human side is equally important. EAPs are installed to provide services for employees and their families, services that help people who are having personal problems. The following statement in an editorial emphasizes the human value of having an employee assistance program:

> EAPs have not, to date, managed to provide neat solutions to the major problems facing corporate survival, but EAPs have provided partial remedies and created new pathways for corporate considerations in terms of work life and employee health.[2]

Employee assistance programs have not eliminated the devastating cost of chemical dependency, but they have served to reduce these costs, a subject covered in Chapter 7. They have also served to improve the quality of work life and create a work environment where the employee's health is an important corporate consideration. This is becoming more evident in organizations that have faced up to the seriousness of drug- and alcohol-related problems in the workplace and have implemented programs in an effort to contain these problems. Not only have troubled employees been helped through EAPs, but organizations have helped themselves in establishing a no-nonsense approach to a problem that many other organizations continue to ignore. Admitting that a problem exists and doing something about it wins the respect of everyone who is potentially affected by the problem. In an organization where five to ten percent of the employee population is experiencing alcohol- or drug-related job performance problems, virtually everyone in that organization is affected in one way or another. Dealing with the problem in a direct fashion reflects an organizational point of view that is both humanistic and employee oriented in nature, and it also reflects a leadership that knows the value of human capital and how to protect that investment.

In the past, few corporate managers would consider investing in anything that could not show a positive cost-benefit ratio. Now they are more likely to measure the social and political consequences of not having a program, and can appreciate the fact that employee assistance programming is a human investment that could also prove to be "profitable." Cost-effectiveness notwithstanding, acknowledging the human side and not just the economic side of the EAP reflects the influence of social and political concerns.[3] The rationale that some organizations offer to defend their EAP investment, however, is quite simple: Employees who feel better also perform better.

Labor-union programs are likely to interpret the program's success in these terms. The United Steelworkers Guide to Rehabilitation

Programs stresses that labor and management share common interests in helping the chemically dependent worker, and that chemical dependency shortens life. Medical evidence indicates that the chemically dependent person's life span is reduced by eight to ten years. In addition, this person is more susceptible to many other illnesses because of excessive drinking and/or drug use. A second cause for common concern, the guide reports, is the progressive nature of the disease. It gets worse with each episode. The prognosis is absolutely certain: illness, physical and mental impairment, and early death, if left untreated. Another point that the guide makes is that both labor and management know the relationship between alcohol abuse and accidents. The chemically dependent person is a safety threat to him/herself and others. All the above are important reasons for labor and management to cooperate with each other in dealing with this problem, but the major concern, the guide stresses, should be the rehabilitation of the chemically dependent person—"to restore this person to a state of self-confidence and health."[4]

The human benefits of the EAP go beyond the rehabilitation of the employee. Helping an employee with his or her problem is helping a family with its problem. Identifying and motivating a chemically dependent employee to seek treatment usually results in treatment for the entire family. Alcoholism or drug abuse is often referred to as a "family disease," the chemically dependent person is merely the "identified patient" within the family unit.[5] This person has been singled out because of unacceptable behavior, a behavior that is both self-destructive and disruptive to the family.

If the EAP refers the employee to a community treatment program, the program is likely to involve the entire family in the treatment process. Most treatment programs provide family therapy for "significant others," and some even urge immediate family members to spend a short time living in the program. If the "identified patient" refuses to cooperate in the family approach to treatment, admission to the program may even be denied. Most inpatient and outpatient services are likely to be flexible on this matter, however.

The concept of the "identified patient" actually has its roots in family theory. It is useful to call the member who carries the symptom the "identified patient," and the identified patient's symptoms serve a family function as well as an individual function.[6] The family behaves as if it were a unit and the term "family homeostasis" refers to this behavior.[7] When one person in a family has pain which shows up in symptoms, all family members are feeling the pain in some way.

Hence, using the workplace and job jeopardy to motivate chemically dependent employees toward seeking treatment has clinical implications and potential benefits beyond the obvious benefits of recovery for the individual. The EAP's value in humanistic terms becomes a quantitative measure in that it reaches several persons in need of assistance. The supervisor receives assistance in dealing with a problem for which there had been no easy solution and the coworker gets help with a problem that was at least a nuisance and at times dangerous. Last but not least, the employee's family gets help with a problem that might never have been addressed were it not for the company EAP.

EAPs FREE UP SUPERVISORS

Troubled employees are time consuming. A chemically dependent person spends a great deal of time doing whatever is necessary to continue to drink or use drugs. This includes being absent, leaving the worksite, being late, extending lunch and morning breaks, and being inefficient. It also includes consuming the time of others such as fellow employees and supervisors. Supervisors who must deal with chemically dependent employees, or more accurately, don't deal with chemically dependent employees, spend valuable time attempting to circumvent the problem. This is especially true in work organizations where it is difficult to fire an employee. Many bureaucratic organizations such as government agencies, hospitals, and other public-sector and voluntary-sector work organizations fall into this group. Work organizations that are unionized are sometimes inhibited by collective bargaining agreements and mounds of paperwork and procedures necessary to discharge an employee who is performing at a substandard level. In a recent discussion I had with a middle-management supervisor about a chemically dependent employee, the supervisor expressed frustration and hopelessness in attempts to resolve the problem. The employee was a union member who continually violated rules and regulations by committing minor infractions. Writing up these infractions would be time consuming in and of itself, but taking the appropriate disciplinary action was even more time consuming. The actual termination of such an employee could take years. In an effort to correct the problem without bringing formal charges against the employee, several intervention interviews were conducted. The employee was counseled informally in the hope that the process of progressive disciplinary action could be avoided. With repeated failures, the supervisor's despair became evident. "If I only had the time," the supervisor complained, "I'd fire this one."

It is difficult to know whether or not the procedures are totally to blame in this instance. The supervisor, perhaps, may not have taken the time to learn what steps to take and may have been experiencing the frustration of inexperience. The troubled employee, nevertheless, can expend a supervisor's time and energies needlessly. While the EAP does not relieve the supervisor of those responsibilities that are a function of the job, it will provide continuous support in resolving highly sensitive and often disruptive employee problems, allowing more time to handle operational duties and accountabilities.[8] One important function of the EAP is training supervisors to recognize and document patterns of deteriorating job performance. With these skills the supervisor is prepared to collect the data necessary to conduct an early intervention interview. An early referral to the EAP will, in most instances, result in a positive outcome. Even if the employee does not respond favorably, the supervisor's action will be an important step in the progressive disciplinary process.

The training provided by the EAP helps the supervisor develop a greater awareness of the impact of personal problems in the workplace—the impact of these problems on morale, health, and productivity. As stated earlier, the supervisor's knowledge about alcoholism and drug abuse is not nearly as important as the ability to identify the troubled employee through patterns of deteriorating job performance. An understanding of the relationship between personal problems and work performance, however, will provide the ability to deal quickly and effectively with both troubled employees and marginally functioning employees.

EAPs ARE GOOD EMPLOYER-EMPLOYEE RELATIONS

An employee assistance program is an employer-sponsored benefit designed to offer employees and members of their immediate families assistance with a wide variety of personal problems. EAPs are a form of indirect compensation, a perquisite or employee service not unlike company-sponsored daycare centers, company paid physical examinations, and social or health club memberships. Many EAPs offer legal advice, help on tax matters, family counseling, psychotherapy, and many services that an employee might otherwise pay for. While chemical-dependency services are likely to be the major function of many EAPs, providing help on other personal matters can be equally important. Having a program that addresses all kinds of personal problems eliminates the stigma of being referred to a program for alcoholism or drug abuse, and offering such a range of services changes it from a program for "those" employees to a service for "all" employees.

Employee assistance programming is simply good employer-employee relations. A program with a wide range of services administered in the best interest of the employee is one way to show that the company cares. The message communicated is that the organization is concerned about its people and has an employee assistance program to prove it. Providing such services is recognition that an employee's problems are also the organization's problems, whether or not job stress contributed to the problem. An employer can find countless reasons for having an EAP but few for not. From a practical point of view one reason is that the employee is a valuable resource and a costly investment that must be protected. From a human point of view, the organization exists in a community and has a social responsibility to the members of that community, including its employees. This responsibility is to identify troubled employees through deteriorating job performance and provide the help necessary to correct the problem.[9] While both "valuable resource" and "performance" are clearly management terms that translate into corporate dollars, this does not diminish the fact that EAPs help employees and/or members of their families—a fact that translates into good employer-employee relations.

Providing employees help with their personal problems reflects a human approach to personnel management that many large and successful corporations have adopted. Most companies, however, pay "lip service" to "genuine people orientation." (It should be noted that most companies also do not have EAPs.) Identifying this as the "lip-service disaster," the authors of *In Search of Excellence* contend that:

> Almost every management we've been around says that people are important—vital, in fact. But having said that, they then don't pay much attention to their people. In fact, they probably don't even realize their omissions. "People issues take up all my time," is the typical rejoinder. What they often really mean is, "This business would be so easy if it weren't for people.". . . Only when we look at the excellent companies do we see the contrast . . . . Caring runs in the veins of the managers of these institutions. . . . Although most top managements assert that their companies care for their people, the excellent companies are distinguished by the intensity and pervasiveness of this concern.[10]

Implementing an EAP will not, of course, transform an organization into an "excellent" company. The formula to becoming an excellent company is somewhat more complicated than that. It involves an orchestration of structural devices, systems, styles, and values. But it may be a contributing factor toward developing a better relationship between employer and employee. Most managements agree that their employees are their most important asset. Giving the employees a program that they can turn to for help is an action that talks louder than words, an action that will benefit everyone involved.

AN EAP IS GOOD PUBLIC/COMMUNITY RELATIONS

Good public relations is another benefit of having an employee assistance program. Many organizations have gone public with their EAPs, boasting the fact that they care enough about their employees to provide them with help for their personal problems. *Time* magazine carried a full-page advertisement by ITT on their EAP, which was direct in its message that chemical dependency is a real and serious problem that corporate America cannot ignore. Using a pictorial of a working man standing next to his pre-teenage son, the ad states, "Who does a 12–year-old turn to when his dad's on drugs?"[11]

The message is that chemical dependency is a problem that affects employer, employee, and employee's family; and that the problem exists right under our noses in business and industry. Most importantly, the ITT ad identifies the workplace as the right place for intervention and the drug abuser as a person who looks just like any other person. Finally, the ad communicates that through their EAP the company has taken responsibility for rehabilitation rather than allowing the problem to run its course, then dumping the ex-employee onto the community to deal with. Using *Time* magazine to reach the employees of a corporation may not deliver the most efficient cost-per-thousand impressions. There are other more economical ways to do internal marketing. This is an excellent way, however, to reach the employees while at home and most importantly, to reach the families of employees. Troubled employees often seek help at the urging of their families, and their families are more likely to take such action when they are aware of a company EAP.

Social marketing is not a new idea. It has been used by businesses and industries for decades to provide the consumer with information, usually as a public service. "Going public" with the company EAP both provides information to the general public about problems in the workplace and places the company on the cutting edge of doing something about them. Unlike some companies that keep their EAPs quiet and others that have no EAP at all, ITT not only confronts the problem head-on, but tells the world about it. The fact that chemical dependency is a serious health problem affecting business, industry, and the community is no secret. Making known the organization's effort to help the troubled employee should not be a secret either. This kind of information goes a long way in shaping a corporate image built on genuine concern and social responsibility.

EAPs ARE GOOD PUBLIC POLICY

"Public policy," an integrative concept that incorporates both "social responsibility" and "corporate social responsiveness," has become an important factor in the decision-making process.[12] Equal opportunity, pollution control, poverty reduction, product safety, and, of course, programs for the health and safety of employees are public policy issues that must not be overlooked by corporate managers and decision makers.[13] Society's expectation that the private sector take responsibility for its environment and its people is expressed through consumer response and through the legislature. Products that are not safe are not being bought and organizations that contaminate the air are being regulated. Companies that discriminate against and/or fire alcoholics and drug abusers are being challenged in the courts. And they are often losing!

Society expects work organizations to give something back to the community that allows it to exist. These "givebacks" come in the form of human services that the community might otherwise have to provide, and go beyond those fringe benefits found in a basic compensation package. Industry is expected to make an aesthetic or social contribution to the environment, polluters are being held accountable for past and present contamination, and all business and industry is being held responsible for the health and safety of their employees. Enlightened work organizations have identified alcohol and drug abuse as health and safety issues and many are responding by implementing employee assistance programs. In 1991, the total number of programs exceeded twenty-thousand. The Federal Drug-Free Workplace Act of 1988 has "encouraged" employee assistance, thereby making EAPs a public policy issue. Private sector organizations receiving federal funding must comply. (See Chapter 4 for more on this subject)

EAPs HELP SET PERFORMANCE STANDARDS

Training company supervisors in the procedures of identifying and referring troubled employees is not only important to the EAP process, it is also important in setting standards for job performance and for improving operational control. Supervisors are the essential link between the employee and the EAP, and training is necessary to ensure their effectiveness in this critical role. The person in charge of the unit, department or division is trained to observe and document job performance, conduct an intervention interview, and take action on the problem. As part of the training the supervisor also learns (or relearns) the organization's policy and procedure on dealing with job-performance problems whatever their cause may be. This is especially important in large, decentralized organizations where policies and procedures may have been modified to the point that different divisions look like different companies. Training serves to reduce these differences by reinforcing company-wide policy and by helping supervisors to deal with job performance problems procedurally, consistently, and effectively. The training not only provides supervisors with the necessary skills to identify the troubled employee, but also reinforces those supervisory skills and techniques essential to day-to-day personnel management. The supervisor comes away with a good understanding of how to address all job-performance problems, including those that are alcohol and drug related.

Training is a three-hour investment of time that is especially important to first-line supervisors. Many supervisors are promoted from the rank and file and continue to identify with former coworkers. While their front-line experience is often an important prerequisite to the job, it can also inhibit the supervisory process. Even if the supervisor had not worked directly with those employees, close identification with a troubled employee may sometimes interfere with taking appropriate action. The first-line supervisor functions in a nebulous place in the world of work somewhere between management and wage earner. Because this person is in a particularly vulnerable position, a structured approach to addressing job performance problems is necessary. As Peter F. Drucker says, "He has now, by and large, become a buffer between management, union, and workers. And like all buffers, his main function is to take the blows." Drucker continues:

> He is separated from the men he supervises by an ever-higher wall of resentment, suspicion, and hostility. At the same time, he is separated from management by his lack of technical and managerial knowledge.[14]

While the supervisor's job will continue to be a difficult one, supervisory training reinforces performance standards and discourages judgment calls based on personal values. A clear understanding of policy and procedure, and an understanding that such problems must be handled consistently, without prejudice, allows the supervisor to do the job confidently. Objectivity, fairness, consistency and decisiveness are emphasized in supervisory training—supervisory qualities that are also valuable in monitoring daily performance.

CREATIVE EAPs FACILITATE EQUAL OPPORTUNITY EMPLOYMENT GOALS

The employee assistance program has a responsibility to reach all employee groups and provide services uniformly throughout the organization. One measure of program effectiveness is, in fact, penetration and program reach. Geographical segmentation, minority divisions, job functions, salary ranges, length of employment, age groupings, gender differences, and any number of categories forming the organization's composition can be targeted. In a corporation that has many different work groups, for example, it is the EAP administrator's job to know what the referral/employee ratio is and whether or not key targeted groups are equally represented. If one group's referral rate is disproportionately low, it could mean that supervisory training is necessary for that particular segment of the organization or that internal marketing strategies should be reviewed.

The EAP may contribute to the organization's efforts to satisfy equal employment opportunity (EEO) efforts. Minority employees and handicapped employees have special needs that are addressed in any effective EAP. An effective program will develop innovative methods to ensure that these groups are reached and that appropriate resources are available to satisfy these needs.[15] This is an area that had been sadly neglected in the past. In 1980 an extensive computerized search of the literature was conducted by a researcher attempting to reference information on industrial alcoholism programs for Latinos and not one reference could be found![16] In the black community, alcohol- and drug-abuse problems have been largely ignored. Ironically, alcohol abuse has been cited as the number one health, mental health, and social problem in the black community.[17] While more recent information shows that some gains have been made in reaching minority groups and women in the workplace, continued efforts are necessary to close the gap. Having an EAP provides an excellent opportunity to correct this problem and provide a valuable service for the organization, the community, and the employees.

EAPs PROMOTE HEALTH AND SAFETY

The EAP may also contribute to the organization's efforts to satisfy standards regulated by the Occupational Safety and Health Administration (OSHA).[18] Not only is OSHA concerned with safety and accidents in the work environment, but it is also concerned with occupational health and illness. Organizations have shown concern for the safety and health of their employees by taking steps to improve the work environment and to make employees more aware of potential problems.[19] Many organizations, in addition to having EAPs also have worksite wellness programs (WWPs). The WWPs provide services and information for employees on all aspects of health and safety including measures to minimize on- and off-the-job accidents. Nutrition education, blood pressure screening, cardiovascular monitoring, exercise programs, and stress management are also WWP functions. The EAP identifies troubled employees through job performance (broadbrush model) while the WWP uses health screenings to identify employees at high risk for illness. A new concept called "megabrush" is being advanced that combines EAPs and WWPs. The objective is to manage them as discrete programs within the organization, but to utilize each other's services conjointly. Researchers suggest that WWPs be structurally separate from EAPs, but organizationally linked, functionally coordinated, and effectively working together.[20]

Alcoholism and drug abuse are not issues concerning only health and illness, but are also safety and accident issues. The use of mood-altering chemicals is responsible for a high percentage of occupational accidents—18,000 are attributed to alcohol use alone. While training supervisors to recognize and refer troubled employees is the primary function of the EAP, educating the employee population about drugs and alcohol use and abuse is also important. Lunch time education programs are popular in many organizations and informational seminars on a variety of safety and health subjects are not uncommon. Many EAPs provide counseling or conduct workshops on overeating and smoking. While some of these activities are functions of worksite wellness programs rather than EAPs, all are relevant to and supportive of OSHA concerns and objectives. The presence of such programs is likely to reduce both the incidences of chemical dependency, as well as the cost of lost productivity related to such problems.

NOTES

1. William S. Duncan, *The EAP Manual* (New York: National Council on Alcoholism, 1982), 11.

2. Deborah J. Comstock, "Employee Assistance Programs: Current Dimensions," *EAP Digest* (May/June 1983): 46.

3. Walter Scanlon, "Corporate Cost-Benefit: Only One Cost Factor Among Many," *The ALMACAN* 14, Issue 6 (June 1984): 3.

4. "Alcoholism: Programs with Promise," Pittsburgh: United Steel Workers of America (offset).

5. LeClair Bissell, *Understanding Alcoholism* (Chicago: Claretian, 1976), 35.

6. Virginia Satir, *Cojoint Family Therapy* (Palo Alto, CA: Science and Behavior, 1967), 1.

7. D.D. Jackson, "The question of Family Homeostasis," *Psychiatric Quarterly Supplement* (1977): 79–90.

8. "The Advantages of EAPs," *Alcoholism/The National Magazine* (August 1984); 26.

9. Randall S. Schuler, *Personnel and Human Resource Management* (St. Paul: West, 1981), 319.

10. Thomas J. Peters and Robert H. Waterman, *In Search of Excellence* (New York: Harper & Row, 1982), 239.

11. *Time* (September 3, 1984), 37.

12. Rogene A. Buchholz, *Business Environment and Public Policy* (Englewood Cliffs, NJ: Prentice-Hall, 1982), xi.

13. Walter Scanlon, "Corporate Cost Benefit: Only One Factor Among Many," *The ALMACAN* 14, Issue 6. (June 1984): 3.

14. Peter F. Drucker, *Management: Tasks, Responsibilities, Practices* (New York: Harper & Row, 1973), 280.

15. Dale A. Masi, *Designing Employee Assistance Programs* (New York: AMACOM, 1984), 155.

16. Ibid., 159.

17. Ibid., 173.

18. John Dolan, "The Staffing Requirements of Employee Assistance Programs," in *Mental Wellness Programs for Employees,* eds. Richard H. Egdahl and Diana Chapman Walsh (New York: Springer-Verlag, 1980), 131.

19. Randall S. Schuler, *Personnel and Human Resource Management* (St. Paul: West, 1981), 319.

20. John C. Erfurt, Andrea Foote, and Max A. Heirich, "The Core Technology of "Megabrush" —Employee Assistance and Wellness Programs Combined," Worker Health Program, Institute of Labor & Industrial Relations, The University of Michigan, September 1990. (Paper in progress.)

16

Legal Considerations and Implications

ISSUES OF DISCRIMINATION

The Federal Rehabilitation Act (FRA) of 1973 prohibits discrimination against any person with a current or former handicap who is otherwise qualified to work. A supplement was added to this important piece of legislation in 1975 qualifying the handicapped individual as a person who (1) had a physical or mental disability that impaired his or her employability, and (2) could be expected to benefit in terms of employability from the vocational rehabilitation services provided under the act.[1] This was later clarified by Attorney General Griffin Bell, who concluded that "Persons suffering from alcohol and drug addiction are included within the statutory definition of 'handicapped individuals.'"[2]

The development of the 1978 Comprehensive Rehabilitation Act Amendment of the Federal Rehabilitation Act of 1973 further reduced the ambiguity in the definition of the "qualified handicapped individual." It insured that alcoholics and drug abusers who were either recovering or in treatment would be protected by the act while quelling fears that airlines and drug companies might be required to hire active alcoholics and drug addicts. The spirit of the amendment excludes those individuals whose:

current use of alcohol or drugs prevents such individuals from performing the duties of the job in question or whose employment, by reason of such current alcohol or drug abuse, would constitute a direct threat to property or the safety of others.[3]

In July of 1990, President Bush signed the Americans With Disabilities Act (ADA). The Act (H.R.2273) protects the following groups against discrimination in employment, public accommodations and publicly funded services: (1) individuals who have recovered from or are in treatment for alcohol and drug problems, (2) qualified individuals with current alcohol problems, and (3) individuals who are erroneously regarded as a current user of illegal drugs. The act does not protect individuals with current drug problems against employment discrimination but does prohibit health care providers, vocational rehabilitation providers, and other service providers from denying services solely on the basis of a person's current drug use.[4]

It should be noted that compliance to the Federal Rehabilitation Act of 1973, to the Americans With Disabilities Act, and to their amendments is applicable to organizations that have government contracts or receive government funding in any form.

While the Americans With Disabilities Act is too new to have any cases to report on, the implications and enforcement of the Federal Rehabilitation Act is best understood in reviewing a case where an alcoholic employee had been fired, *Ruzek* v. *General Services Administration (GSA)*. In that case GSA fired the employee, a guard, for sleeping on the job. The employee appealed the action contending that the charge was related to his alcoholism, a problem he presently had under control. The decision to fire the employee was upheld on appeal nevertheless, the presiding official concluding that GSA had met its obligation by telling the employee at an earlier disciplinary hearing that assistance was available if he wanted it.

This decision was also appealed by the employee, this time to the Merit Systems Protection Board (MSPB), the administrative authority charged with adjudicating federal employee appeals from a variety of employee-initiated actions, and the following decision was rendered:

> Thus we find that, in order to afford reasonable accommodation to an employee who is handicapped by alcoholism, an agency must offer the employee rehabilitative assistance and allow him an opportunity to take sick leave for treatment if necessary, before initiating any disciplinary action for continuing performance or misconduct problems related to his alcoholism. In offering rehabilitative assistance, the employee's supervisor need not confront him with the supervisor's belief that the employee has a drinking problem, but he must make the employee aware in general terms that the supervisor suspects the employee has a problem affecting his performance or conduct, and that the supervisor recommends that the employee participate in a par-

ticular rehabilitation or counseling program which is available to
him.[5]

A critique on this case concludes that the board found GSA's "weak
attempt at counseling" did not constitute "reasonable accommodation," and that the "agency should have cancelled the proposed firing
and given the employee another chance."[6]

The significance of this case is that it underscores the importance of
having an *effective* employee assistance program—a program that
includes training supervisory personnel. First, the supervisor would
have had a better understanding of the organization's policy and
procedure and would have skillfully avoided discussing the
employee's drinking. As the board ruling stated, "he must make the
employee aware in general terms" that he suspects a problem exists
that is affecting his job performance. Second, the supervisor would
have been trained in the technique of constructive confrontation interviewing, discussing only the employee's deteriorating job performance and offering the EAP as a means to a solution. Third, just as the
incidents of poor job performance were noted, the offer of assistance
would have also been documented and the employee advised that
continued job performance problems could lead to disciplinary action
and/or firing. If the employee's performance improves to a satisfactory level, with or without the help of the EAP, then the supervisor's
problem is solved. If the employee's performance continues to decline,
however, such as by sleeping on duty, then the disciplinary action
could be carried out. GSA would have met its obligation of
"reasonable accommodation" by formally offering the employee help
and by giving him time to bring his performance to an acceptable
level. Chances are that the employee would have accepted the offer,
job performance would have improved, and the charge of sleeping on
the job might not have ever occurred.

A report on the importance of an EAP's function and its concomitant benefits when considering the legal protection afforded
the chemically dependent person on matters concerning disciplinary action and discharge is emphasized in the *St. John's Law Review*.
It states that:

The modern view as to the prerequisites to discharge of an
alcoholic [drug abuser] employee, as outlined by arbitrator Lewis
Kesselman, is:

(1) That the employee be informed as to the nature of his illness.
(2) He must be directed or encouraged to seek treatment.
(3) He must refuse treatment, or

(4) He must fail to make substantial progress over a considerable period of time.[7]

Without an effective employee assistance program in place, most
companies could not carry out these prerequisites before discharging an
employee. Managers, supervisors, and human resource practitioners
have not studied the subtleties of dealing with the troubled employee,
nor do they know the legal implications involved. It is the business of
the EAP to have this information and to train supervisory staff in
applying it. Not only will an EAP protect the employee from being
discriminated against as a "qualified handicapped individual," but it
will also protect the employer from otherwise unnecessary and costly
litigation. If an organization has an effective EAP it is almost assured that
"reasonable accommodation" will be afforded the employee, and that
the employee will have to accept the help or pay the consequences. The
consequences for a chemically dependent employee will be a progression of the illness, continued deteriorating job performance, and, ultimately, termination. Fortunately, most employees will accept the
treatment alternative, arrest their dependence on alcohol and/or drugs,
and become productive employees once again.

LEGAL CONCERNS ABOUT EAPs

While having an EAP in place may serve to protect both the
employee and the employer, it may also introduce legal and ethical
issues that might not otherwise concern a work organization. An EAP
could serve to reduce the chance of legal action against an employer,
insuring that the company policies on alcohol and drug abuse are
followed, and that the supervisors are trained to deal with such issues
competently. Providing such services without *competent* legal counsel
would be ill-advised, however, and could render the organization
vulnerable to legal entanglement. When a work organization implements an employee assistance program and provides rehabilitation
services for the chemically dependent employee, it should also consider the issue of compliance with federal and/or state statutes
designed to protect that employee. While most organizations are
not legally required to comply with such statutes, following the
guidelines set forth in federal anti-discrimination acts and in confidentiality codes is simply a good practice. But EAPs in the private
sector that follow these guidelines *too* closely will limit their ability to
function optimally.

As discussed in earlier chapters, explicit confidentiality concerns
are governed by a "final rule" promulgated in 1987 for programs that

provide "alcohol or drug diagnosis, treatment, or referral for treatment and which are federally assisted, directly or indirectly."[8] This final rule was written primarily for the guidance of federally funded treatment programs, not EAPs.

The Federal Rehabilitation Act of 1973, when applicable, protects handicapped persons from discrimination while other federal laws and regulations govern the confidentiality of drug and alcohol abuse patient records.[9] These include Title 42 Code of Federal Regulations, Section 408 of the Drug Abuse Office and Treatment Act, the Comprehensive Alcohol Abuse and Alcoholism Prevention Act of 1970, and the Privacy Act of 1974.[10] Many state governments also have fair employment laws and privacy acts with varying criteria of compliance.

While any corporation might unwittingly (or wittingly) find itself in violation of those sections of the Rehabilitation Act of 1973 that protect the "qualified handicapped individual" from discrimination (Sections 503 and 504), an organization with an employee assistance program in place may be more vulnerable. On the one hand, the EAP and the company that has done its homework will be aware of the act and all of its implications. It will be sure not to violate the employee's rights. On the other hand, any organization that is providing "treatment" has entered an arena where the litigious employee can more easily support a claim of discrimination. Not being referred to the company EAP for treatment, for example, is frequently cited in cases where the chemical-dependent employee was not afforded "reasonable accommodation" to get help. Making an incorrect assessment of the employee's problem or not referring the employee to an appropriate treatment facility may also provide grounds for litigation and/or recompense.

AIDS AND THE WORKPLACE

Acquired Immune Deficiency Syndrome (AIDS) is the plague of the century. From a few cases in the early 1980s, AIDS is now an epidemic that is virtually eliminating segments of society. Several industries have been hit hard by this devastating illness and its exponential potential is not yet fully known. The world of fashion, dance, and art continues to fall victim to this complex illness. In between bouts with pneumonia, Kaposi's sarcoma, and other opportunistic infections, the AIDS patient's primary treatment is counseling. While employees who are HIV (Human Immunodeficiency Virus) positive are frequently referred or refer themselves to the EAP, AIDS-related problems, like other troubled employee problems, are beyond the scope of this book.

But because AIDS can be transmitted through contaminated needles and intravenous drug users are at high risk, there are related legal concerns.

Employees who, through deteriorating job performance, have been identified to have both illnesses—AIDS and drug addiction—are protected under federal, state, and local laws against discrimination and violations of confidentiality. In addition to those protections afforded through the Federal Rehabilitation Act of 1973 and the Americans With Disabilities Act, additional legislation is frequently proposed and introduced in both the Senate and the House of Representatives. It is incumbent upon the work organization to be up-to-date on new legislation that, while intended to protect the person with AIDS, may be a factor in determining disciplinary and/or treatment decisions for chemically dependent employees with AIDS. The Chevron Corporation, in its guidelines for dealing with AIDS-related employment issues, advises on the importance of such matters:

> Remember, when dealing with employees who have AIDS, that they may be covered by the laws and regulations that protect handicapped people against discrimination. Additionally, some cities have passed laws specifically prohibiting discrimination against employees with AIDS. The Human Resource Staff should be consulted before making any employment decisions regarding employees with AIDS.[11]

Chevron recognizes the importance of addressing such problems in a professional and humanistic manner. A professionally staffed employee assistance program is important to both helping persons with AIDS and training supervisors in how to handle AIDS–chemical dependency issues.

ISSUES OF CONFIDENTIALITY

Discrimination against the "qualified handicapped individual" might be either minimized or exacerbated by the presence of an EAP—depending on the program's legal savvy and the professional care by which such services are offered. As stated above, there need not be an EAP present for an organization to find itself on the wrong end of a discrimination case and in violation of the federal or state statutes and codes. A confidentiality case may be a different matter. The federal and state statutes and codes that insure the confidentiality of drug- and alcohol-abuse patient records usually apply to health care professionals. If the EAP has a licensed health care professional, the possibility of such a violation, albeit remote, may exist. As noted earlier, however, most private-sector employers are exempt from the federal government's "final rule" on confidentiality. Besides, confidentiality rules do not offer the protection from disclosure that might be expected. Client records can usually be successfully subpoenaed if the counselor is not licensed and therefore cannot classify client sessions as "privileged."[12] Many EAP counselors, while they may be credentialed professionals (CEAPs, CACs, etc.), may not be licensed in the legal sense. Nevertheless, the federal government, through both the Congress and the Department of Health and Human Services, has addressed the issues of confidentiality. Knowing this, it is advised that those persons involved in the administration of EAPs be aware of federal statutes and regulations governing the confidentiality of patient records.[13] Title 42 of the Code of Federal Regulations on confidentiality is one such regulation that protects patients (or the employees) who are being treated for alcohol or drug dependence.

Obviously, having an employee assistance program means opening the company's door to a host of legal concerns that might not otherwise be present. Not only does this include those discussed above, but it also includes related legal problems, such as counselor negligence, for which the organization may or may not be liable.[14] Virtually any clinical decision can be challenged and any qualified professional could end up on the wrong side of a malpractice suit. While this is not a common occurrence in the field, it should not be dismissed as an insignificant concern.

SCREENING EMPLOYEES FOR DRUG USE

Another area of concern for organizations with EAPs is the question of drug screening in the workplace and its legal implications. This is a very gray area and the legality of such practices is not yet very clear. A report on the subject published in *The ALMACAN* (now the *EX-CHANGE*) labeled drug screening as an "anathema to EAPs" and to civil rights.[15] Routine drug screening does not sit well with EAP practitioners and firing an employee on the basis of a positive drug finding might be in violation of existing policies if the organization has a program. While a positive toxicology finding may be used to disqualify an employee if that test is used for enforcement purposes only, this may constitute a violation of the "reasonable accommodation" rule if the organization *does* have a program in place. A positive toxicology report should, in that case, result in a referral for counseling and treatment and not in termination.[16] Many work organizations and government agencies with employees in safety sensitive positions, however, are not bound to this seemingly logical decision. In both the federal Department of Transportation (DOT) and the Department of Defense (DOD), mandatory drug testing programs are in place. Some local agencies will allow chemically dependent employees treatment if they voluntarily seek assistance through the EAP, but employees who test positive through random, medical, or for-cause testing programs are terminated.

Further complicating the issue of drug screening in the workplace is the question of reliability of the results. The Centers for Disease Control and other agencies responsible for monitoring the performance of drug-screening laboratories have conducted proficiency testing of a number of laboratories nationally. The false positive rates they actually found ranged from 5 percent to 28 percent.[17] According to a report published in the *Journal of the American Medical Association*, laboratories using urine screening tests to detect the presence of methadone, barbiturates, amphetamines, cocaine, and other drugs are "yielding unreliable results." A study was conducted based on 100 urine samples containing small amounts of various drugs sent to 13 laboratories that serve a total of 262 methadone treatment centers. The researches reported that 91 percent of the laboratories had unacceptable false-negative rates for barbiturates, 100 percent for amphetamines, 50 percent for methadone, 91 percent for cocaine, 15 percent for codeine, and 92 percent for morphine![18]

This report was released in the mid-1980s, however, and laboratories have since improved on both their technology and on "chain of custody" monitoring. Laboratories in the 1990s have demonstrated considerable improvements on the accuracy of test results, using enzyme immunoassays (EIA) for routine testing that are then confirmed by gas chromatography-mass spectrometry (GC-MS). This is also cost effective in that only positive results are confirmed by the more expensive second test.

Nevertheless, an administrative judge who is aware of the possibility of inaccuracies, and not convinced that the confirmation methods used today are virtually error-proof, will probably rule in favor of the employee. Only if the employee is in a safety-sensitive position, or if other evidence supports the toxicology findings, will the ruling favor the employer. While upon appeal an occasional case may be overturned, it is better to err on the side of societal safety than on job protection.

KNOWING THE RULES

Legal considerations notwithstanding, the employee assistance program is more likely to protect than expose the organization to legal entanglement. Federal and local statutes, laws, rules, regulations, and guidelines are written to protect those who might otherwise have their rights violated. Such protections are very specific, however, and mandated compliance is a matter of understanding their application. It is always advisable, therefore, that the work organization and the EAP have legal counsel available to ensure compliance and protect all concerned from the possibility of violation.

NOTES

1. The Federal Rehabilitation Act, U.S.C. 706 (5), 1975 Supp.

2. Griffin B. Bell, "Opinion of the Attorney General of the United States," 43, op. No. 12 (April 12, 1977): 3–10.

3. Janet Maleson Spencer, "The Developing Notion of Employer Responsibility for the Alcoholic, Drug-Addicted or Mentally Ill Employee: An Examination Under Federal and State Employment Statutes and Arbitration Decisions," *St. Johns Law Review*, Vol. 53, No. 4 (Summer 1979): 34.

4. "ActionWatch," May 1990, Legal Action Center, New York.

5. Merit Systems Protection Board (MSPB) Docket SL075209017, August 20, 1981.

6. Dale A. Masi, *Designing Employee Assistance Programs* (New York: AMACOM, 1984), 172.

7. Spencer, "Developing," 701.

8. Richard Bickerton, MS, CEAP, "The Right To Privacy, The Need To Know: Are They Natural Enemies?," *Exchange*, EAP Association, Inc. (Arlington, VA, March 1990), 42.

9. The Federal Rehabilitation Act of 1973 (Title 29 of the U.S. Code, Section 701 *et seq.*) as recorded in "Employment Discrimination And What To Do About It" (New York: The Legal Action Center, 1982), 2.

10. Legal Action Center, "Confidentiality of Alcohol and Drug Abuse Patient Records," in *Confidentiality*, a compilation of articles from "Of Substance" (New York: The Legal Action Center, 1984), 2

12. Bickerton, "Privacy," *Exchange*, 42.

11. The Chevron Corporation, "Guidelines For Handling Issues Related To AIDS," submitted by John P. O'Connell, July 1990.

13. Frank B. Wolfe III and Marthanda J. Beckworth, "Confidentiality of Employee Records in Employee Assistance Programs," *EAP Digest* (December 1982): 34.

14. John T. Gorman and Lorraine C. Stapples, "*Counselor* Negligence and Exposure to Liability," *The ALMACAN*, 12, Issue 3 (Arlington, VA: Association of Labor-Management Administrators and Consultants on Alcoholism, March 1982), 9.

15. Dick Stanford, "Drug Screening: Anathema to EAPs, Civil Rights," *The ALMACAN*, 4, Issue 7 (Arlington, VA: Association of Labor-Management Administrators and Consultants on Alcoholism, July 1983): 3.

16. Richard C. Boldt, Staff Attorney, Legal Action Center, letter dated June 1, 1984.

17. Legal Action Center, "Of Substance" (New York: Legal Action Center, April 1984), 1.

18. Occupational Health & Safety Letter (April 22, 1985).

External Employee Assistance Programs

WHY GO EXTERNAL?

An employee assistance program, internal or external, can be described as a cost-effective, confidential, early intervention system designed to help employees with problems that interfere with their ability to function on the job. The work organization's objectives in implementing a program remain the same whether the service is delivered in-house or contracted to an outside provider, that is, cost containment and problem resolution.

Proponents of in-house programs will usually agree that any organization with more than three thousand employees should have an internal EAP. Such a program will generally cost the organization between $25 and $50 per employee per year, depending upon the scope of the program. There are other variables, however, that the organization must consider before installing a program. One such variable is the location of these "three thousand employees." If they are at several different plants or offices, then the in-house program might not be practical. Traveling between worksites can be time consuming for both the EAP practitioner and the employees being served.

Another consideration is the management style and the corporate culture of the organization, such as, what is important to the organization, how does the organization work and how does the organization do things? As discussed in Chapter 14, if the EAP does not fit in, its effectiveness will be limited. A situation audit should be carefully conducted to determine whether or not an in-house program will be the most effective alternative, both pragmatically and economically. If the organization decides instead to have an external EAP, then there are essentially two choices: establishing a program through an *EAP Contractor* or joining an *EAP Consortium* of cooperating organizations.

THE EAP CONTRACTOR

More than half of the workforce in the United States are employed by organizations that have a total employee population of fewer than five hundred people. The EAP Consultant evolved out of the need to reach those organizations that employ between thirty and three thousand people as well as larger organizations with a dispersed, mobile, or otherwise hard-to-reach workforce. This includes, but is not limited to, work settings that are long distances from corporate headquarters and employees who frequently move between geographical areas such as sales persons and transportation workers. The National Institute of Alcohol Abuse and Alcoholism makes a distinction between employees that are hard-to-reach occupational groups in terms of problem identification and groups that are hard-to-reach in terms of service delivery:

> [The hard-to-reach work force is] the universe of employed and self-employed workers, who, for various reasons, have not been (or cannot be) serviced by traditional organizational alcoholism programs; this group may include members of the dispersed work force, the mobile work force, and selected other professions.[1]

Some employees may be hard-to-reach in terms of both problem identification *and* service delivery. Long-distance bus drivers and interstate sales representatives, for example, can avoid early problem identification and would not benefit from the traditional "job jeopardy" model. Even when the problem is self-diagnosed the employee would not have easy access to assistance if the EAP is located at corporate headquarters. Other types of work groups such as physicians, lawyers, engineers, and so on, are usually accessible but protective relationships among colleagues may hinder the identification process. Alcohol and/or drug dependence can often progress undetected to the point where these employees or professionals are no longer employable.

THE ROLE AND FUNCTION OF THE EAP CONTRACTOR

While the EAP Contractor model may not be the final solution in reaching the hard-to-reach workforce, it provides a degree of flexibility and adaptability not usually found in in-house programs. Most EAP Contractors will tailor a program to the needs of the organization and provide those services that will best serve the organization's objectives. Companies with in-house EAPs sometimes contract out to design programs that will service those worksites not easily accessible. Airlines, multi-plant manufacturing companies, brokerage houses, and any organization large enough to have an in-house program might contract with an external EAP as well to service its branches and smaller subsidiaries.

While the range of services provided may vary from one EAP Contractor to the next, the operational structure and the method of service delivery usually follows one of two models: centralized and decentralized. The centralized model will operate out of one location with all communications coming through that office. This includes support services such as developing internal marketing strategies, evaluating program performance, designing supervisory training programs, and conducting education programs for employees. The central office deals directly with the organization it is serving and all referrals, self and supervisory, are processed here. This does not mean that the troubled employee actually goes to the central EAP, but that a telephone interview is conducted and the employee is then referred to a local "affiliate" for further assessment and/or referral. Many centralized models have toll-free telephone numbers to insure twenty-four–hour service and affiliates located throughout the country ready to respond to employee needs. Sometimes called "stringers," these affiliates are generalists who are trained to assess a range of personal problems. They provide long- and short-term counseling services and know the community resources within their geographical area including detoxification and rehabilitation facilities for employees who are chemically dependent. The affiliates seldom, if ever, have contact with the employer, their function being limited to providing clinical and social-work services. If the employee is a supervisory referral, a clinical liaison at the central EAP monitors job performance and communicates relevant information to the affiliate assigned to the case. The clinical liaison also communicates with the employee's supervisor or corporate liaison that information necessary to facilitate treatment. This information is limited, of course, by whatever federal and/or local confidentiality statutes apply.

The decentralized EAP also has a central office where much of the clinical, management, and marketing strategies are developed, but it has full-service satellite EAPs strategically located to serve their geographical areas. These geographical areas might be major cities or locations convenient to client organizations. The number of personnel located at a satellite EAP may vary; at some locations there may be only one or two EAP generalists present. Unlike the affiliates of the centralized model that are retained on a fee basis for services provided, the satellite EAPs usually have salaried staff members who work directly with the organizations that they serve. They provide a complete range of EAP services including counseling employees, training supervisors, and conducting education programs for the employee population. The satellite EAP is decentralized in that it operates as an independent EAP for the organizations it serves. In terms of management structure, it is sometimes considered a separate unit for profit accounting purposes, not unlike a "strategic business unit" (SBU) or a "profit center" (PC) of a corporation.

The centralized and the decentralized EAPs are also known as "long-distance external" and "local-external" EAPs, respectively.[2] As discussed above, one model directs all operations from a central EAP while the other model operates locally. Still others might operate as both centralized and decentralized EAPs. They may have local-external EAPs in major cities but may also have toll-free telephone numbers for those employees who are not within the geographical areas served. An EAP that is contracted to provide services for a manufacturing firm may have a local-external EAP near the firm's corporate headquarters, for example, but must also be accessible to the firm's large sales staff. The long-distance external EAP model is added to meet this need.

STAFFING AN EXTERNAL EAP

The components of both internal and external EAPs are essentially the same. The EAP must have a strong administrative component, clinical component, education/training component, and a research/evaluation component.

The administrative component is divided into management and personnel functions. This person(s) is the business manager, the program manager, the staff supervisor, the marketing director, the policy advisor, the legal liaison, the insurance negotiator, and the company strategist. The person in this role must have the business acumen necessary to communicate with client organizations, be able to interpret corporate policies and procedures, understand and be able to communicate the concepts of employee assistance programming, have a working knowledge of research methods, understand clinical issues and their application in the workplace, and be capable of training and supervising trainers.

The research/evaluation component is important to an internal EAP but essential to an external EAP. This person is an expert in quantitative methods and data application. An EAP Contractor might be doing a great job for the organizations it is operating programs for, but when it is time to renegotiate the contract, the proof of the pudding is in the figures. Research and evaluation is also necessary to remove those "bugs" that are adversely affecting operations. Internal marketing strategies can be monitored through evaluation, and ineffective "affiliates" can be reviewed through quantitative and qualitative performance appraisals. Macro and micro studies are developed by the EAP researcher to improve on the program's existing methods of operation and to make contributions to the field of employee assistance programming.

The educational component is the mind of the EAP and the clinical component is its heart.[3] The person responsible for training company supervisors and conducting employee education programs must both understand clinical concepts and be able to talk business language. A business organization will not tolerate for long a trainer who comes to the organization spewing social work or psychological jargon. The supervisor needs help not confusion in dealing with the troubled employee.

The function of the heart of the EAP—the clinical component—will vary, depending upon its scale and scope. Larger EAPs may employ a number of specialists who limit their responsibilities to one or two functions.[4] A staffing pattern could include a credentialed addictions counselor, a certified social worker, a clinical psychologist, and a board certified psychiatrist all trained in chemical dependency, family matters, gambling problems, eating disorders, or nonclinical issues such as legal matters and financial issues.

In a small local-external EAP, an EAP generalist might be responsible for the entire operation. An EAP generalist is a jack-of-all-trades, able to do assessments and referrals, marketing, counseling, training, education, and ongoing maintenance functions for client organizations. The advantage to the generalist approach is that credibility and communication is enhanced in that client organizations only have one person that handles all of their EAP needs. The problem in the generalist approach, however, is that EAP jacks-of-all-trades are hard to find and training is time consuming and costly.[5]

THE SERVICES PROVIDED

The range of services provided by an external EAP varies with the scope of the operation and the type of contractual service agreement. There are three core functions, however, that are inherent in any full-service agreement. They include program design, program implementation or installation, and program maintenance. Program design is the developing and shaping of a program to fit the subscribing organization's needs. This not only includes the obvious tasks such as assisting the organization in developing a company-wide policy and implementing internal marketing strategies, it also includes conducting a situation audit, examining the culture of the organization, reviewing existing policies and procedures, and designing a program that will complement the philosophy and management style of the organization. In this way the external EAP is similar to the internal EAP in that it is developed specifically for that organization. The program's objective is also the same: to reduce the cost of alcohol- and drug-related problems and other problems that interfere with the employee's ability to function on the job.

Program implementation is the process of moving from the drawing board to the bricks and mortar. All program components should be in place, a policy statement will have been formulated, procedures should be operational, and EAP staffing assignments have been made. Supervisory training sessions should have already begun, internal marketing strategies have also begun, and all parties should understand their role in the system. Conflicts in existing personnel policies will have been settled, insurance coverage has been determined to be adequate, and, if the EAP is local-external, a suitable location has been secured. If the program is long-distance external, there should be affiliates wherever the company's employees may be. The EAP should be able to handle any employee crisis before the ink on the contract dries.

Effective program maintenance will follow good program design and implementation. Problems can be expected during the implementation period, but if these problems are not solved within a short period of time, then the design and/or the implementation should be reviewed. If the supervisory referral rate is low, for example, then more supervisory training sessions are probably necessary. If the self-referral rate is low then program promotion strategies should be reviewed, or the scope of services available should be expanded.

Maintenance is sometimes described as anything that happens between program implementation and program evaluation. Evaluation is actually a function of maintenance, a function that separates the excellent programs from the sea of mediocre programs. In this age of computer technology, a client organization should be able to review an EAP's activity on short notice. While cost-benefit studies are difficult and costly to conduct, cost-effectiveness studies are usually included as per the contractual agreement. The difference between the two, as discussed in earlier chapters, is that although both are quantitative, cost benefit measures dollars saved while cost effectiveness is a relative measure such as the total number of employees reached, and so on.

EAP services provided can be divided into three basic categories: organizational services, employee/client services, and general program consultation.[6]

Organizational services are indirect services, that is, all services that do not involve the troubled employee directly. These would include policy development, supervisor training, marketing plans, research/evaluation, developing a labor/management advisory committee, general employee education programs, training a company liaison, and so on.

Employee/client services are direct services or all services that are provided for the troubled employee/member and his or her family. This includes assessment, counseling, referral services. It also includes direct consultation with union representatives and supervisors on identified troubled employee concerns.

General program consultation might include any limited contractual service. Assisting an organization in designing and implementing an internal EAP, for example, or training supervisors in the supervisory referral process would be considered general program consultation.

THE ADVANTAGES OF AN EXTERNAL EAP

One advantage of an external EAP is that it allows a smaller company to have access to a multidisciplinary staff. Where a large corporation might be capable of staffing an internal EAP with specialists, including a certified social worker, credentialed alcoholism counselor, and such, the small organization is likely to be limited to one EAP generalist. The generalist would assess and refer but not treat or counsel troubled employees. While most EAPs provide only assessment and referral services, some do short-term counseling and treatment. Long-term treatment is not an EAP function.

Another argument for an external EAP is that confidentiality violations, real or perceived, are less likely. The EAP is away from the worksite, an important factor in generating referrals. Confidentiality of record is also assured since the EAP, rather than the work organization, owns the records.

Malpractice and liability suits are avoided with an external program. The EAP Contractor assumes full responsibility for treatment and case management, a condition that should be stipulated in the contract. Other advantages include the ability to reach a dispersed population, 24–hour coverage, no vacations to interfere with program continuity, affordable full-service costs, and an improved potential for servicing management-level employees. Finally, in contracting for

EAP services rather than having an in-house program, the organization stays out of the EAP business.

THE DISADVANTAGES OF AN EXTERNAL EAP

In-house programs have a higher rate of supervisor referrals. Most employees seen in-house have been referred by supervisors while self-referrals account for most employees seen in external programs. In-house program advocates argue that supervisors prefer to work with company staff while external EAPs claim that their supervisory referral rate is not lower but that their rate of self-referrals is simply higher. External programs do, in fact, have a lower rate of supervisory referrals.

Leaving the worksite to go to the EAP might be an inconvenience for some employees. Not all employees seeking assistance are job jeopardy cases and many of these employees would prefer the convenience of in-house assistance. While most employees would prefer the anonymity that an external program affords, some may not be concerned. It should be noted that many in-house programs also provide this anonymity if their EAP is located off site.

The external EAP Contractor is viewed by the client organization as a professional consultant, a status unique to external practitioners. As a consultant, however, its role will be limited to those functions identified in the contract. It is not likely to become an integral work group of the organization operating within and as a part of the corporate culture. This is not to say that the utilization rate will not be high, but that the external EAP is a service to and not a department in the client organization.

THE COST OF THE EXTERNAL EAP

Fees for services are as varied as the services offered. Sometimes referred to as a "capitation fee," a full-service contract may range anywhere between $16 and $114 per employee in the organization, the top and bottom rates being extremely rare. Most larger EAP Contractors fix their rate between $30 and $72 per annum or between $2.50 and $6 per month. A capitation fee of $35 for an organization of two thousand employees, for example, will cost the employer $70,000 per year. A "utilization rate" is sometimes included in the contract and if the referrals exceed that rate, a surcharge or add-on fee is assessed.

If an EAP Contractor is called into an organization for general program consultation services only, an hourly rate would usually apply. Consultation fees could range between $75 and $250 per hour depending upon the contractual time and services agreed upon.

Some EAP Contractors may offer services on a per visit or a per service basis. If the organization is billed per employee visit, a minimum "retainer" fee is sometimes required. Training supervisors how to identify and refer troubled employees may have a separate fixed rate per training session.

External EAPs may be found in both non-profit and for-profit sectors. Non-profit EAPs may receive grants or supplemental funding from third-party sources, consequently, their rate may be lower. While such EAP contract with both private business public service organizations, for-profit EAPs are more likely to serve private business and industry. Whether the EAP is non-profit or for-profit, the employer, association, or organization served pays for the program. In joint union-management programs, management is usually expected to pay most if not all costs. Employees are seldom, if ever, billed for direct services provided by the EAP. If the employee is referred for treatment, however, this becomes a matter between the treatment provider, the insurance available, and the employee. If it becomes necessary for a chemically dependent employee to be hospitalized in a 28–day rehabilitation program, for example, the EAP is not responsible for the cost of this treatment.

SHOPPING FOR AN EXTERNAL EAP

The organization in search for an external EAP must become a sophisticated shopper. There are a number of ways in which a second-rate EAP Contractor can underbid a reputable EAP Contractor, all adding up to compromising the quality of care.[7] Most organizations exploring the feasibility of an EAP have no experience in making such an investment. While personnel managers and medical administrators have a conceptual understanding of employee assistance programming, they are likely to have had little or no training in the field. It is advisable, therefore, that a task force be formed that includes individuals whose collective experience will insure the best possible selection. This task force should include representatives from finance, personnel and medical departments, the union, and a special effort should be made to find someone who has a working understanding of EAPs. If possible, a recovering chemically dependent person might be included. Retaining an independent general program consultant who will not be bidding for the contract is also advisable. Without a frame of reference for comparison, it is impossible to know how to cost-out the services provided. The independent consultant can be important here. The task force should read whatever information is available on the subject and meet with other organizations that have external EAPs. Only in this way will they be able to ask the right questions and fully understand the implications of the replies.

It is essential that the task force conduct site visits. The purpose is to observe and understand how a troubled employee is processed when he or she visits the EAP. In visiting one major EAP, I was particularly impressed by how quickly I was ushered from the reception area to a private waiting room. The EAP was apparently in the habit of protecting the confidentiality of the employees they served.

Criteria for selecting a EAP Contractor fall into four broad categories: track record, product (services), costs, and staff.[8] It is important to learn who the EAP Contractor's current clients are, what the comparative costs for comparative services are, and how the EAP staff is qualified to do the job. In reviewing the types of services offered, it is important to determine which of the two EAP models discussed above would best serve the organization's needs. A local-external EAP (decentralized) might be best for some organizations while a long-distance external EAP (centralized) may meet the needs of others.

The following checklist is recommended when assessing the qualifications, competence and potential effectiveness of an EAP Contractor:

How long has the EAP Contractor been in business?

Are they in any other business? Is there a potential conflict of interest? (One advantage of an EAP Contractor is that it is, or should be, their only business.)

What are the credentials of the staff?

How are the services delivered (telephone or personal contact)?

Is there a systematic follow-up? What are the service control mechanisms?

Will there be a good fit? Is the prospective subscriber too large or too small for the EAP Contractor?

Is there a sophisticated management information system in place? Will the EAP Contractor provide cost-benefit and/or cost-effectiveness analyses?

Who are the current clients? What are the turnover and renewal rates?

What is the EAP Contractor's philosophy of service? Do they provide direct services or do they assess and refer for treatment? (Direct services are included in the contract but services through community providers are usually paid by the employee or through insurance.)

THE EAP CONSORTIUM ALTERNATIVE

Since the word "consortium" is associated with matters of a financial nature, it is appropriate that this word be used to describe organizations that come together to form a common employee assistance program. An EAP Consortium is described as a cooperative agreement among companies and agencies that do not have enough employees to warrant their own separate EAPs.[9] The most basic difference between an EAP Contractor's model and an EAP Consortium is that Consortium is owned by its client organizations and a Contractor is not. The Consortium is governed collectively by the member organizations and assumes full responsibility for all services provided. The EAP Contractor is owned by the contractor.

Many of the advantages associated with the contracted EAP are also applicable to the Consortium. These include affordable full-service rates, a staff of EAP specialists, confidentiality safeguards, continuity of service, and a better chance to reach higher-level employees. Like the contracted EAP, the EAP Consortium is likely to have a higher rate of self-referrals than the in-house program. In addition, the Consortium model is available to those organizations that may be even too small for an EAP Contractor to service.

The disadvantages, however, are also similar to those of a contracted EAP. Supervisors are less likely to refer to an external EAP, even though it is owned in part by the organization. The utilization rate for employees with chemical-dependency problems, consequently, may be lower then that of an in-house program.

THE EXTERNAL EAP IN CONCLUSION

There are several good reasons why external employee assistance programs are in a growth period. First, most employees in the United States work for small organizations creating many more opportunities for external EAPs. Second, "managed health care" has become an important focus of the 1990s and most external EAPs have very strong managed health care components. Many EAP Contractors are, in fact, marketing their services as managed health care products. While employee assistance is a functional objective, the focus today is more on reducing the escalating costs of health care benefits expenditures.

Third, organizations with dispersed employee populations cannot be served effectively with an in-house program. Even organizations with in-house EAPs in place sometimes contract for additional services in order to reach otherwise unreachable employees. These might include dispersed or mobile employees, employees not within the geographical area, or employees not likely to use an in-house program.

The external EAP is an alternative to the internal model. It is a viable alternative in many instances and is very often the only logical alternative. The decision to go external should be based on information that makes that the best model, of course, but so should the decision to go internal. While all the variables discussed should be considered before making the choice, choosing an external EAP is not an irrevocable decision. Some organizations, in fact, purchase a one-year contract to learn more about the EAP concept. At the end of that year they may decide either to renew the contract or apply what they have learned and build an in-house EAP.

NOTES

1. National Institute on Alcohol Abuse and Alcoholism, "Target: Alcohol Abuse in the Hard-to-Reach Work Force" (1982): 23.

2. Ann B. Sudduth, "Assessing Employee Use of Internal and External Employee Assistance Programs for Alcohol and Control Group," in *EAP Research: An Annual of Research and Research Issues,* 1, C, ed. Howard Grimes (Troy, MI: Performance Resource Press, 1984), 26.

3. John Dolan, "The Staffing Requirements of Employee Assistance Programs," in *Mental Wellness Programs for Employees,* eds. Richard H. Egdahl and Diana Chapman Walsh (New York: Springer-Verlag, 1980), 132.

4. Susan K. Isenberg, "EAP Service Center Model" in *The Human Resources Management Handbook/Principles and Practice of Employee Assistance Programs,* eds. Samuel H. Klarreich, James L. Francek, and C. Eugene Moore (New York: Praeger, 1985), 62.

5. Ibid.

6. Ibid., 60, 61.

7. James Offield, " Buyer Beware," *Employee Assistance* (Waco, TX: Stephens Publishing, November 1988): 41.

8. Howard V. Schmitz, *The Handbook of Employee Counseling Programs* (New York: The New York Business Group on Health, 1982), 59.

9. Dale A. Masi, *Designing Employee Assistance Programs* (New York: AMACOM, 1984), 61.

18

Summing It Up
and Sorting It Out

BACK TO THE BEGINNING

Altering one's state of conscientiousness, some social scientists agree, is an innate, normal drive. Like hunger and sex, it is a basic human need that, if not satisfied, will preclude normal development. Drugs, some theorists believe, are merely one means of satisfying this drive.[1]

Many might take exception to this idea. Yet one does not have to look far for evidence supporting this hypothesis or the premise from which it was advanced. People seek out ways to feel good—in essence, to alter one's state of consciousness—by jogging, going to a movie, sitting in a hot tub, riding on a roller coaster, or exploring the underwater world. A glass of wine, a line of coke, or a marijuana cigarette are obvious methods used to alter consciousness. Even children, three and four years old, commonly enjoy an altered state of consciousness by whirling themselves into vertiginous stupors. A few years later they may discover that hyperventilating by breathing heavily, then having another child squeeze their chest will produce a lightheadedness or cause them to faint.[2]

The point here is that people do enjoy changing their moods even from an early age. Describing this as an "innate, normal drive" does, indeed, seem to apply when we consider all of the options available to the pleasure seeker. Some methods employed to achieve this objective are exploratory, others are perfectly harmless, and still others have the potential for abuse. Mood-altering chemicals—alcohol and other drugs—are most likely to fall into the latter category.

While most people who use alcohol or other recreational drugs do so socially without creating problems for themselves or others, a large minority develop alcoholism or become dependent on such substances. These individuals, and the problems created by them, are found in the community, in the family, and, of course, in the workplace. The profile of the chemically dependent person and the choice of substances used and abused may vary from one decade to the next, but the measure of the problem's impact on society and in the workplace remains the same: human lives and economic losses.

WHOSE RESPONSIBILITY ARE THEY?

The responsibility for solving the problem has traditionally found itself squarely in the lap of the community. Employees who found themselves in trouble with alcohol or other drugs were fired and society had to pick up the cost of both shelter and treatment. The corporate sector, for the most part, did not see this as their problem. Their objective, after all, is to realize profit not to solve social problems. Solving social problems was a function of the voluntary and public sectors, not the business sector. Some companies, however, while no less economically motivated, began to offer help to troubled employees. These companies realized, in fact, that helping troubled employees and maximiming profit were not mutually exclusive objectives. On the contrary, they are complementary objectives.

This realization marked the beginning of help for the troubled employee. First came counseling with a focus on ending active drinking in the workplace, followed by the introduction of a more formal program approach inspired by the success of Alcoholics Anonymous. Occupational alcoholism programs as well as the entire alcoholism treatment community rejoiced in 1956 when the American Medical Association declared alcoholism a disease. In 1987 another important resolution was announced. The AMA resolved that all drug dependencies, including alcoholism, are diseases and that treatment is a legitimate part of medical practice. Both decisions were important steps toward removing the stigma associated with the chemical dependency.

The shift from occupational alcoholism programs (OAP) to employee assistance programs (EAPs) came in 1965 when the National Council on Alcoholism (NCA), now called the National Council on Alcoholism and Drug Dependence (NCADD), stressed the importance of job performance in achieving early identification of the alcoholic employee.[3] This was an important shift in strategy that also served to diminish the stigma associated with alcoholism. It became evident that employee assistance programming was here to stay. Industry and business had realized the potential benefits of an effective EAP.

A chronology of those factors that contributed to and influenced the growth of employee assistance programming is shown in Chapter 3. Some of these, The Hughes Act, for example, deserve repeating. Also known as the Comprehensive Alcohol Abuse and Alcoholism Prevention, Treatment, and Rehabilitation Act, it provided federal funding for state programs. It made the concept of employee assistance programming a public policy issue.

The coming together of labor and management was both an event and a change in attitude. Acknowledging chemical dependency as a problem of concern for all, and influencing a cooperative effort to resolve the problem, joint union-management programs were formed.

Special interest groups of Alcoholics Anonymous such as lawyers' groups, physicians' groups, and intervention groups for airline pilots made it easier for reticent work organizations to admit that they too have employees with chemical dependency problems. Politicians, presidents' wives, actors and actresses, sports heroes, and rock stars have brought chemical dependency out of the closet, emphasizing the importance of treatment and underscoring the success of rehabilitation efforts.

The corporate and labor communities have responded to date with approximately twenty thousand employee assistance programs serving millions of employees throughout the United States. In addition, there are other alternatives to in-house programs such as joining an EAP consortium of smaller companies that subscribe to an existing service, or contracting with an EAP contractor or vendor.

THE ORGANIZATIONS THAT DO

The value and benefits of employee assistance programming are documented throughout this text. Terms most used to express these values include cost containment, improved employee relations, high morale, cost benefit, recovery, occupational health and safety, humanistic concerns, corporate social responsiveness, family benefits, and improved job performance. While there are few, if any, negative concerns in a well-administered EAP, there are several planning considerations. They include but are not limited to program cost, organizational structure, corporate culture, organization size, legal constraints, and union input, if applicable.

Some organizations, the literature suggests, provide EAP services for altruistic reasons. Others look for a positive dollar value, viewing the EAP as a work group that will prove its worth in economic terms.

Many organizations believe it to be their social responsibility to provide such services and still others consider it an investment in human capital.[4] The majority of organizations with EAPs in place would probably agree, however, that their rationale for offering such services is a mix of all of the above.

The employee assistance program also serves to encourage a human relations approach to human resource management. It opens the door to a management style that benefits both employer and employee. It is a human approach to a costly problem that can work effectively in any organization if administered properly. This is not to say that a corporation will or should abandon its "rational" management style and adopt a human relations management style.[5] The EAP is, in fact, a rational approach to a serious problem that is most effective in such organizations. The benefits of an EAP—both economic and humanistic—can be realized even in a company that adamantly defends the position that its only objective is to "make as much money as possible for its stockholders...so long as it stays within the rules of the game."[6] The fact notwithstanding that society has tightened these rules, the cost-reducing benefits of an EAP may actually facilitate that objective.

The EAP's objective is to help troubled individual with their problems and return them to the job as full functioning employees. This transition can take place on all levels of the organization and may include union or nonunion workers, line or staff employees, management or non-management personnel. In the process of achieving this goal the EAP makes other contributions to the organization. It helps set standards of behavior and provides guidelines for management and supervisory staff to carry out these standards. Policies are established to deal with the problems associated with chemical abuse in the workplace and procedures are formulated to deal with those employees whose job performance has been affected by alcoholism and/or drug dependence. The 1988 Drug Free Workplace Act and the 1990 National Drug Control Strategy are encouraging that federally funded work organizations provide such services.

The EAP is more than a service for troubled employees. It is a work group within an organization that can shape human resource management policy and strategy. While this may appear to be the proverbial "tail wagging the dog," management's decesion to implement a program can influence policy. The scope of the problem and the cost to the employer makes chemical dependency a management issue with a high priority.

The advocate for employee assistance programming can argue the benefits of the EAP ad infinitum. It promotes policies and standards on drug and alcohol use and abuse, as well as on other troubled-employee problems affecting job performance. Supervisors and managers are trained to address these problems appropriately, gaining confidence and credibility in their role. Lost productivity, absenteeism, and poor job performance are reduced and troubled employees become productive employees. Sharp reductions in tardiness, long lunches, and early quitting incidents are likely. Reductions in on- and off-the-job injuries as well as in the number of disability claims and compensation applications filed have been reported. Reduced insurance premiums and/or payments for employee medical expenses are realized. A well-managed EAP is a primary managed health care function.

The EAP may serve to improve employer-employee relations. Charges of discrimination against the "qualified handicapped individual" may even be avoided. Concern for the employee's health and welfare is demonstrated and improved union-management relations are likely. Employee education programs on drinking, drug use, and related issues serve to create a company-wide awareness of chemical dependency as a health problem.

THE ORGANIZATIONS THAT DO NOT

Many organizations choose not to address drug- and alcohol-related problems in a systematic or programmatic way. One reason may be that they have not yet learned about EAPs and the value of their function. Or, perhaps, the potential benefits may be known but no one has proposed the idea to management. Some corporate managers still maintain the illusion that no such problems exist in their organization. Other companies may practice a management style that leaves no room for what they may believe are clinical solutions to problems that, in management's view, call for disciplinary action. Many organizations are simply so poorly managed that chemical dependency in the workplace is the least of their problems.

Some organizations have, undoubtedly, examined the pros and cons of employee assistance programming, concluding that the payoff would not justify the investment; that the EAP with all of its concomitant benefits would not do much for their organization. From a cost containment point of view, it might be cheaper to fire than to rehabilitate employees. This may be especially true where the employees are unskilled, or where the capital investment tied up in an EAP might realize a better return somewhere else. Finally, some organizations may simply rule out the concept as not being cost effective.

THE EAP AS A MANAGEMENT FUNCTION

The cost to business and industry is billions of dollars annually, a cost ultimately passed on to the consumer. Governmental influences, including the Drug-Free Workplace Act and federal drug testing mandates, have underscored chemical dependency as a serious workplace concern. It is a prioity concern that deserves a place in the strategic planning process; a pervasive and insidious problem that is not likely to disappear without a planned course of action. Taking no action is, in a sense, a decision to tolerate alcoholism and drug abuse as long as the employee can get away with it. This means that the organization will ignore the problem until job performance deteriorates to the point where the employee is no longer functioning and termination is inevitable. The organization may even have a written policy on dealing with alcohol and drug use on the job, but without provisions for troubled employees, the policy is meaningless.

Attempting to mandate a chemical-free employee population through drug testing and disciplinary action alone is not realistic. Managing alcohol- and drug-related problems in the workplace has two equally important parts. One part is a firm policy and enforceable penalties for employees who violate rules on use and/or possession of alcohol and/or drugs on the job. The second part is a policy and procedure for helping troubled employees with problems that interfere with their ability to function on the job. Choosing to manage one part and not the other is like choosing to manage only half of the organization's investments. The other half is, in fact, responsible for the greater share of those costs associated with the "multi-billion dollar hangover." Like that majority of the iceberg that is under water, this is the part that should not be ignored.

While the absolute cost of chemical dependency to the organization might be hidden under various categories, the effects of the problem on human resource management, employer-employee relations and employee morale cannot be hidden. Yet most companies have neither formulated a workable policy on chemical dependency nor implemented an EAP. Some, perhaps, never will. Nevertheless, the concept remains a dynamic approach to a serious problem affecting industry and business. Increasingly, the issue discussed by management today is not whether or not to implement a program addressing the problems of alcoholism and drug abuse in the workplace, but rather how to go about doing it.

STEPPING UP TO AN EFFECTIVE PROGRAM

The following is a step-by-step recapitulation of implementating a program (see Figure 18.1). The first step is *Designing the EAP System*. This involves determining what will be necessary to meet the organization's basic needs. The intended scope of the program and the size of the organization will determine the number of EAP staff members necessary to do the job, and the disciplines from which they should be recruited. An EAP in an organization that has employees throughout the country will be designed differently from a program serving one location. An external EAP might be contracted to serve work locations not accessible by the in-house EAP. The physical location of the program as well as the organizational level of functioning are equally important to the program's success. The union(s), where applicable, should be invited to participate, and an advisory committee of labor and management representatives formed to govern operations. Community treatment resources and insurance coverage must be secured before the first referral is made to the EAP. The design of

Figure 18.1 Building the EAP

the EAP should facilitate an interfacing of management, union, and employee population with the program and the program with the community resources necessary to the success of the system. The EAP, like any other capital investment, should be researched, planned, and designed to insure optimal effectiveness and efficiency.

The organization must *Formulate Policy and Procedures* if it expects to do the job right. A policy statement from the CEO is essential, confidentiality requirements must be established, and procedures for program utilization should be available. This is the single most important task in that it governs the entire system and protects all involved.

Management and Administration is managing all the functions and responsibilities of the program. This includes maintaining an organizational position conducive to fulfilling the EAP's objectives, insuring that there is adequate insurance coverage for employees needing treatment, implementing and maintaining a record-keeping system, maintaining malpractice liability insurance, and hiring a qualified EAP staff. The administrator must also review existing personnel policies and attempt to eliminate any conflicts. In a small EAP the counselor, the trainer, and the administrator may be the functions of one person.

Marketing the Program means more than advertising the program. The objective of any marketing effort is ultimately to actualize an exchange between the service provider and the prospective client. In this case the EAP is the provider and both the employees and the supervisors are the clients. In order for these clients to "buy" the EAP services, these services must fulfill a need. It is essential, therefore, that the EAP know what these needs are, and offer whatever is necessary to meet them. It is equally important that the employee population and the supervisory staff learn what their own needs are. Through education and training this is accomplished and the need for services is "created." The EAP is then ready to use whatever media are available to promote the services offered.

Supervisory Training is critical to the EAP's success. As discussed in earlier chapters, it is not as important for the supervisor to understand chemical dependency as it is to know how to make a referral to the EAP. On-site training sessions should be planned and conducted on a regular basis and procedures should be distributed to all supervisory personnel.

Employee Education, as suggested above, is an important step in constructing an EAP. The employees learn that the EAP is an employer-sponsored benefit designed to offer a variety of services for employees and their family members. As the program gains acceptance among the general employee population, the number of self-referrals increases and a level of trust is established. This makes it easier for the supervisor to make a referral and for the troubled employee to accept a referral.

Evaluation and Research is an ongoing function. Data collection provides the program with information necessary for clinical and program studies.

Modification and Review allows the EAP to develop and change as needs change for both the organization and the program. Community resources and treatment data are scrutinized, and program modifications are made that best serve both employee and employer. Because objectivity is important here, an advisory committee is importment.

THE EAP IS A SYNERGISTIC FUNCTION

The employee assistance program is the single most effective approach to reducing alcoholism and drug abuse in our society. It is a conduit to the best of treatment resources available, using the threat of job loss as a lever to encourage treatment as an alternative to continued chemical abuse and dependency. In using the job as a treatment tool, the employer precipitates a crisis that the troubled employee must attempt to resolve. Most employees will accept the EAP alternative rather than risk disciplinary action and termination.

Electing to install a company EAP is a decision that is easy to justify. Most programs can demonstrate a positive cost-benefit ratio using sophisticated analysis methods and many more can prove cost savings using estimates and projections. Going beyond such finite measures of success, the EAP's value can also be expressed in humanistic, political, and social terms. An EAP providing a range of services for employees and their families is an invaluable asset both to the community and to the company.

There are countless opportunities for an individual in the world of work that do not exist for those who are unemployed. Not only is it a place where the means to survive are secured, but it is also a place where social needs, personal ambitions, and individual achievements are realized. In a ranking of what employees most want from their jobs, a "sympathetic understanding of personal problems" scores a high third, only behind a "full appreciation for work done," and "feeling 'in' on things." "Good wages," surprisingly, ranked fifth and "tactful disciplining" ranked tenth![7]

Among other things, one could conclude from these findings that there is a basic need to feel secure ("appreciation" and "feeling in"), followed by a need for assistance when one is feeling insecure ("sympathetic understanding"). Is it any wonder, then, that the EAP in helping employees solve personal problems would be especially successful when these personal problems are affecting job security? Chemical dependency is one such problem and the solution to the problem, both for the employer and the employee, can be found right in the workplace. The supervisor and the EAP counselor form a team effort that places the employee on notice while, at the same time, providing an opportunity to get help. The team is threatening to take away the employee's means of support if assistance is not accepted and job performance does not improve. Ironically, the threat of job loss becomes humanistic when that threat is instrumental in treatment and recovery.

The organizational value of the EAP is synergistic. The threat of job loss and the availability of help for personal problems each have separate values. But it is the combination of these separate values that provides a powerful tool serving organizational objectives. It is here that two different systems come together to solve both the economic and human costs of chemical dependency and other personal problems. One system's objective is behavior modification and stress management while the other system's objective is cost containment and productivity. The EAP is a combination of these objectives, restoring the troubled employee both to full health and full productivity. In a well-administered program there will never be a conflict because the bottom line will always be the employee's job performance. The organization's objective in installing an EAP is, after all, to reduce the cost of personal problems affecting job performance. While "humanism" and "concern" should not be dismissed as irrelevent to this objective, neither should they obscure it. The EAP is, in fact, an expression of humane pragmatism.[8] Its goal is both functional and pragmatic. That goal, in simple terms, is to keep the competent worker working. In achieving this goal it also restores the competent worker to good health.

NOTES

1. Andrew Weil, *The Natural Mind* (Boston: Houghton Mifflin, 1973), 19.

2. Ibid.

3. "Target: Alcohol Abuse in the Hard-to-Reach Work Force" (Rockville, MD: National Institute on Alcohol Abuse and Alcoholism, 1982), 3.

4. Carl J. Schramm, "Evaluating Occupational Programs: Efficiency and Effectiveness," in *NIAAA Research Monograph-8/Occupational Alcoholism: A Review of Research Issues* (Washington, DC: Government Printing Office, 1982), 368.

5. Thomas J. Peters and Robert H. Waterman Jr., *In Search of Excellence* (New York: Harper & Row, 1982), 29.

6.   George A. Steiner, John B. Miner, and Edmund R. Gray, *Management Policy and Strategy*, 2nd ed. (New York: Macmillan, 1982), 81.

7.   Paul Hersey and Kenneth H. Blanchard, *Management of Organizational Behavior: Utilizing Human Resources*, Third Edition (Englewood Cliffs, NJ: Prentice-Hall, 1977), 47.

8.   Harrison M. Trice quoted by John McVernon, "Defining the Perimeters of EAP," *The ALMACAN* (Arlington, VA: Association of Labor-management Administrators and Consultants on Alcoholism, April 1984): 8.

Index

About the Author

WALTER F. SCANLON is a management consultant with fifteen years experience in the fields of chemical dependency treatment, employee assistance programming and marketing. He has published widely in the areas of marketing health care services, employee assistance programming, public relations and chemical dependency treatment and wrote the first edition of this book. Mr. Scanlon holds a Master of Business Administration, is a Certified Employee Assistance Professional (CEAP), and a Credentialed Addiction Counselor (CAC). Mr. Scanlon lives in New York City.